Little Fish Big Ocean

Little Fish Big Ocean

**A BUSINESS STUDENT'S GUIDE TO SEPARATING
FROM THE REST OF THE SCHOOL**

Jonathan Buehner

With Guest Authors
Bob McDonald US Secretary of Veterans Affairs, Retired CEO of Procter & Gamble
Bob Morrison Former CEO, 3M, Kraft, Quaker Oats
Tim Koegel Founder, the Koegel Group
Sharon Williams Professional Résumé Writer, Founder of Jobrockit.com
Mark Liston Director, Glass Doctor
Garrett D'Ottavio Brand Manager, Unilever, L'Oreal

Ryan Baise Managing Editor

ISBN: 1508664757
ISBN 13: 9781508664758
Library of Congress Control Number: 2015903341
CreateSpace Independent Publishing Platform
North Charleston, South Carolina

Overview

Foreword

Congratulations! You made it!

You walked across the stage, shook the principal's hand, received your diploma, and survived high school. The last four years were a journey filled with successes and failures, great friends, and unforgettable memories. You've reached the finish line, but the race is far from over.

Starting Blocks at the Finish Line

The next leg of the race is longer, more challenging, and filled with thousands of worthy competitors. (Not that we are trying to scare you or anything!)

Getting accepted to college may have seemed like the culmination of all your hard work and dedication, and in some respects, it is. But that acceptance marks the beginning of a new chapter in your life and brings with it a series of new challenges.

Whether you are starting at a small liberal arts college or a major university with tens of thousands of talented students from all over the world, new people with a myriad of strengths and weaknesses will surround you. Learn to recognize yours. (Yes, you too have weaknesses, even if your mom doesn't think so.)

If you're taking the time to read this book, you are already starting down the right path. Your goal isn't just to graduate; it isn't to be average. Your goal is to be the best version of yourself. Set your standards high. Work to obtain the education and experience that will give you an advantage when applying for a coveted job or an elite MBA program.

Setting the Course

Few students enter college already knowing what they want to do when they grow up. (Here's a little secret: few *adults* know what they want to do when they grow up.) If you're reading this book and feeling a little lost and confused, you are far from alone. Knowing exactly what you want is not nearly as important as the process itself.

Think of college as a road trip with an undetermined destination. Don't get overwhelmed by thoughts of where you will end up or what you will do with your life. Instead, focus on the process and on developing the skills that will make you successful, regardless of the path you choose.

Over the course of this book, we will identify several checkpoints for your journey. With the help of some seasoned professionals, *Little Fish, Big Ocean* provides insight necessary for setting yourself up for success.

Most college students experience a "sink or swim" sensation when they're tossed into a bigger sea with more experienced fish. *Little Fish, Big Ocean* helps students thrive by providing information not taught in the classroom. We want to help you set yourself apart from the rest of the school. But remember, it's up to you to develop your individualized plan and execute it effectively!

America operates as a meritocracy; those who excel are rewarded accordingly.

CHAPTER 1

Maximizing Your Talents and Passions

Don't Stress Out—Seriously

Regardless of the school you attend, one of the most stressful decisions of your freshman (or sophomore) year is selecting a major. Some students enter college knowing exactly what they want to do. Others find themselves in the midst of their fifth major change, rivaling Tommy Boy for most time spent on campus. And while it's great that you're taking time to find your true passion, a college education generally doesn't come cheap, and your indecision can be costly. Find your balance.

Think of your major as an empowering, not imprisoning, decision. Your major acts as a set of guidelines; it helps provide a valuable skill set and can open doors for you, but by no means is it a restriction. Countless successful business professionals have majored in areas ranging from English to music to chemistry. Your major will not curtail your ability to achieve your goals, so please eliminate this sense of fear.

Confusion: The Root of the Problem

Lack of understanding is a primary reason undergraduates have a tough time selecting a major when they first step on campus. With so much new information being thrown in their direction, it's easy to see how students get lost in the weeds.

In an effort to shed light on the dim-lit confusion felt by many students, we have put together some simple explanations of the most common paths for business students. As you read these descriptions, think about whether the field matches your passions, talents, and career aspirations.

Accounting

Accountancy is the system of recording, verifying, and reporting the value of assets, liabilities, income, and expenses in the books of the account. Managers, lenders, investors, tax authorities, and other decision makers use this financial information to make resource allocation decisions between companies, organizations, and public agencies.

The American Institute of Certified Public Accountants (AICPA) goes on to define accounting as "the art of recording, classifying, and summarizing in a significant manner and in terms of money, transactions, and events which are, in the least, of financial character, and interpreting the results thereof."

To put it simply, as an accountant, your job is to keep accurate records of business metrics (e.g., sales, inventory, assets, and profits) and ensure the company's compliance with state, federal, and international regulators.

Finance

The field of finance refers to the concepts of time, money, and risk and how they are interrelated. The task of corporate finance is to provide a company with the funds to operate. Finance majors may choose to pursue careers in corporate financial management, commercial banking, investment banking, or consulting, just to name a few.

A financial professional seeks to find the funds (money from investors) to invest in new projects that will help the company grow and provide a return to both the company and investors. Additionally, corporate finance professionals report and analyze the company's performance while providing projections on how they believe the company will perform in the future. There are many different and complicated functions of finance that offer a wide variety of career opportunities.

Economics

Economics is the social science that studies production, distribution, and consumption of goods and services. Economic analysis is applied throughout society in business, finance, and government, as well as crime, education, family, health, law, politics, religion, social institutions, war, and science.

Economics is the study of the choices people make when incentives and resources influence them.

Marketing

Marketing is creating, delivering, and exchanging offerings (e.g., products, goods, or services) that have value for customers, clients, partners, and society at large. The field of marketing is typically seen as a creative industry responsible for advertising, distribution, and selling, as well as being concerned with the future needs and wants of the customers.

An easier way to define marketing is to think of it as all of the activities associated with the transfer of goods from the producer or seller to the consumer or buyer: advertising, shipping, storing, and selling.

Management

In all business and human organization activity, management is simply the act of getting people together to accomplish desired goals. Management comprises planning, organizing, staffing, leading, directing, and controlling an organization or effort for the purpose of accomplishing a goal. Resourcing encompasses the deployment and manipulation of human resources, financial resources, technological resources, and natural resources.

Management is a broad major with a wide variety of career paths—often pulling individuals from other functions to serve in a leadership role.

Public Relations

Often referred to as "PR," public relations is a liaison between an organization and the public. PR gains an organization or individual exposure to their audiences using topics of public interest and news items that do not require direct payment. Public relations places exposure in credible third-party outlets; it offers a third-party legitimacy that advertising does not have. Common activities include speaking at conferences, working with the press, and employee communication. A number of specialties exist within the field of public relations, such as analyst relations, media relations, investor relations, or labor relations.

PR can be used to build rapport with employees, customers, investors, voters, or the general public. Almost any organization that has a stake in how it is portrayed in the public arena uses some level of public relations.

Entrepreneurship

Entrepreneurship is the practice of starting new organizations, or revitalizing mature organizations, in response to identified opportunities. Entrepreneurship is often a difficult undertaking, as a vast majority of new businesses fail. Entrepreneurial activities are substantially different depending on the type of organization that is being started. Entrepreneurship ranges in scale from smaller, part-time projects to major undertakings that may create many job opportunities.

A Happy Marriage of Passions and Skills

When making your selection, it is important to choose a major with career opportunities in which you would excel and that you would enjoy. If you are having trouble finding one that matches both, follow your passion. Improving your skills is much easier than trying to make yourself passionate about a career path or profession.

Problems often stem from college students not knowing the skills necessary to excel in certain majors and, subsequently, in their desired careers. There's a cloak of mystery surrounding the jobs and the career paths available to specific majors.

Below are lists and descriptions of careers you may choose to pursue depending on the major you select. The goal here is to dispel some confusion by identifying the skill sets that traditionally lead to future success in certain majors.

- Do you enjoy working in teams?
- Are you good with numbers?
- Do you consider yourself an analytical person?
- Are you detail oriented and organized?
- Do you enjoy solving problems?

- Do you enjoy traveling and meeting people?
- Are you good at working with new technology and programs?
- Are you a faster learner?

If you answered yes to most of these questions, a career in *accounting* or *finance* may be a good choice for you.

- Do you enjoy creating models and testing them?
- Do you think theoretically?
- Do you enjoy evaluating problems within a structured framework?
- Do you enjoy studying and analyzing different choices?
- Are you interested in the "big picture"?
- Can you reason critically?

If you answered yes to most of these questions, a career in *economics* may be a good match for your skill set.

- Do you have strong people skills?
- Do you enjoy selling ideas, products, or concepts?
- Do you consider yourself a creative person?
- Are you a strong communicator?
- Are you able to easily identify trends?

If you answered yes to most of these questions, a career in *marketing* or *public relations* may be a good selection.

- Are you a strategic thinker?
- Are you capable of identifying strengths and weaknesses in people?
- Do you enjoy teaching and motivating?
- Are you enthusiastic?
- Are you looking for a major that will give a broad base of career options?
- Do you enjoy working with other people?

If you answered yes to most of these questions, a career in *management* may be a good fit.

Overlap and Opportunity

As you read over the questions above, you probably saw some overlap. Many of the desired skills, such as being a good communicator, having strong analytical skills, or working well with other people, are needed in a number of different business functions.

Although certain fields of study require a particular set of skills, your end goal should always be to continue to grow as a business professional. The most successful people in the business world have the ability to work cross functionally. Leaders in every field have the ability to read and analyze financial statements, communicate their ideas with top management, manage their direct reports, contribute to marketing campaigns, and sell their products or services to the consumer. This might sound daunting, but before you become the top dog, you'll start your career in a specific discipline. A dream career doesn't happen overnight.

How many times have you said to yourself, "Okay, I'm a finance major; what kind of job should I aspire to when I graduate?" Many students are unaware of different career opportunities associated with each major. The first step is to understand the nature of each major and the skills needed to excel. Let's take a look at some options for your first job after receiving your diploma.

Careers in Accounting

An accounting degree can be very beneficial; it helps students develop a useful skill set and provides a structured career path and terrific job opportunities. Each year hundreds of accounting majors choose to start their careers at a prominent accounting firm such as Deloitte Touche, PricewaterhouseCoopers, Ernst & Young, or KPMG.

Any of these firms is a great place to start your career. You will undoubtedly gain valuable experience while earning a competitive starting salary, usually upward of $60,000 for top candidates.

Let's dive down a little deeper. Generally, four broad paths exist for accounting majors:

- Auditing
- Financial accounting
- Management accounting
- Tax accounting

Auditing

"To audit" literally means to "examine or verify." As an auditor, you check and verify that accounting ledgers (books used to record company transactions) and financial statements are correct. Your job may be to audit your own company, another company, or the government. Using random sampling models, you are able to analyze and understand how the company makes money, and determine if their records are correct.

Financial Accounting

Financial accountants prepare financial statements (used to report the financial position and performance of the company). They are generally involved with strategic business decisions, including mergers and acquisitions and long-term financial budgeting.

Management Accounting

A primary responsibility of management accountants is to make capital budgeting decisions. This entails deciding where to spend the company's capital, and how much. Capital, simply put, is the money contributed by investors, plus the money made by the company's operations. This capital is then used for new projects and current expenses.

Management accountants participate in cost analysis and ensure that the company's money is being spent efficiently and responsibly.

Tax Accounting

As might be expected, tax accountants prepare corporate and personal tax statements for companies and individuals. Knowledge of the United States' seventy-four-thousand-page tax code (as of July 2014) can save companies and individuals millions of dollars through deductions and special tax incentives. The demand for tax accountants is high, and positions typically pay well. The individual who wants to be an accountant is required to have a thorough understanding of the specific business, economics, and the federal and state tax codes. Individuals with a strong legal background (JD), coupled with a strong understanding of accounting (CPA) and the tax code, are highly sought after by top companies.

It's important to understand your employment options before you graduate. A number of possibilities exist:

1. Public accounting firms. They are a partnership of professionals who provide accounting services for individuals, businesses, and governments.
2. Government. Accountants work at all three levels (local, state, and federal) to create budgets, analyze costs, and track programs.
3. Corporations. Companies of all sizes need accounting departments to keep specific financial records and report the performance and position of the company.
4. Solo. Some accountants decide to work independently. This requires a sense of entrepreneurship and the ability to generate your own business.

Below is a listing of the requirements to become a certified public accountant (CPA). The view of most business professionals is that a CPA is essential to excelling in the accounting profession and opens up a wide spectrum of career opportunities.

CPA requirements[1] are as follows:

- A bachelor's degree
- 24 semester units in accounting-related subjects
- 24 semester units in business-related subjects
- 150 semester units (or 225 quarter units) of education
- Passing the uniform CPA exam
- One year of general accounting experience supervised by a CPA with an active license
- Passing an ethics course

Hopefully this section has given you a better understanding of the accounting degree and profession. Continuing on, we will explore a variety of career opportunities associated with other business majors, allowing you to assess the major that is best for you.

---

1 http://www.calcpa.org/content/licensure/requirements.aspx

Careers in Finance

Success in finance requires a similar skill set to accounting. Strong analytical skills, the aptitude to solve complex problems, and the ability to communicate ideas are essential for a career in finance. A finance degree provides students with broader, somewhat less-structured career opportunities, ranging from consulting to corporate finance to investment and commercial banking. In reality, the possibilities are endless.

For the sake of brevity, we will focus on four broad-based career paths in finance:

1. Corporate finance
2. Commercial banking
3. Investment banking
4. Consulting

Each of these professions is quite different from the next, despite fitting under the large and somewhat ambiguous finance umbrella. By breaking these career options into four fields, we can identify the skills necessary to excel and the job possibilities traditionally made available in each profession.

We should note that a strong understanding of financial concepts is beneficial in a wide variety of jobs and careers paths; therefore, your career options are not limited to the ones presented in this text. Rest assured; upon graduation you will possess a skill set that opens the door to a wealth of opportunity and the ability to switch careers if your first pick turns out not to be the right fit.

1. Corporate Finance

So you think a job in corporate finance might be your cup of tea, but you're afraid of becoming a corporate bean counter. Let's take a look at the wide spectrum of job opportunities available in the realm of corporate finance.

Many entry-level corporate finance professionals complain that their work is often low-level and mundane. In part, this is because early job responsibilities often involve crunching numbers and organizing data. Despite this stigma, remember that everyone has to pay his or her dues. Managers will recognize a job well done, even when it's a simple task. Be patient and continue to work hard. When you have the opportunity to take on a larger project, run with it, and hit it out of the park.

Successful corporate finance professionals have the following skills:

- The ability to work with others to solve complex problems
- Adaptability to a dynamic business climate
- Strong communication and presentation skills
- Proficiency with changing technology, using these advances to make themselves more efficient employees
- Strong initiative to drive business strategy

Corporate Finance Job Options

Financial Analyst

Financial analyst is a broad-based position with a range of responsibilities, including short- and long-term financial planning, evaluating projects, assisting with mergers and acquisitions, the sale or purchase of assets, and determining how to effectively use financial derivatives to mitigate or eliminate risk for a company.

Risk Analyst

A risk analyst analyzes a wide spectrum of business risks that may affect a specific project, business unit, or a corporation as a whole. These risks include, among others, credit risk, foreign currency risks, sales risk, demand risk, and supply risk. Essentially, the job of a risk analyst is to determine what could go wrong and the probability of that occurrence; the risk analyst then makes recommendations based on his or her analysis.

Cash Manager

Cash manager is a detailed-oriented job associated with handling the cash needs of a business. Cash managers ensure the cash on hand meets daily business requirements (such as bills and payroll) and manage short-term credit needs.

Investor Relations (IR)

IR requires proficiency in finance, coupled with knowledge of public relations or communications. Job responsibilities include communicating with the company's external investors and issuing press releases to explain company policies or events.

Benefits Analyst

A benefits analyst works to find cost-effective benefits for company employees. He or she is responsible for working with human resources to set up and manage things such as pension -fund accounts for employees.

Real Estate Analyst

Real estate analysts find and evaluate real estate opportunities for a business. A strong background in finance and a keen understating of the real estate market are important.

Treasurer

The treasurer is a financial officer responsible for fiscal planning, cash management, and the buying and selling of the company's assets. The position requires strong analytical skills; the treasurer must take into account the company's financial position and the state of the economy to make critical business decisions. In a global company, a successful treasurer should have knowledge of foreign currency and understand how to hedge against potential fluctuations.

Controller

Working as a controller requires a strong background in accounting (many corporate controllers have experience with one of the Big Four accounting firms). Controllers generally develop financial planning models, track financial progress, and establish systems to control and safeguard the company's cash.

These are some, but definitely not all, of the job possibilities in corporate finance. Many corporations have leadership programs that rotate and train you in different financial functions, providing you with a broad-based experience and the opportunity to find out what you enjoy.

Hopefully you noticed many of the financial positions overlap with other business functions (e.g., benefits analyst working with human resources or investor relations needing a strong background in public relations). This should be comforting to those of you who are interested in finance but may not see yourself working solely in the finance world. The ability to work cross functionally is a valued skill in today's dynamic and fast-paced business environment. Corporate finance jobs can offer college graduates great training in the finance discipline.

2. Commercial Banking

Let's step outside the corporate world and take a look at another possible route: commercial banking. Generally, when we think of banking, two things come to mind: Bank of America and *The Wolf of Wall Street*. First, let's touch on the former (more on the latter still to come).

If the daunting ninety-hour workweek as an investment banker isn't your cup of tea, but a career in banking still sounds appealing, commercial banking may be a good fit. Commercial banks offer a variety of job opportunities at the branch and corporate levels. Banking presents the opportunity to exercise a financial skill set and build relationships with clients in both B2B (business-to-business) and B2C (business-to-consumer) capacities.

Successful commercial banking professionals have the following skills:

- Strong people skills and the capability of building and maintaining relationships
- A strong financial skill set and a broad-based understanding of business
- A hint of a salesman (we're not talking about used-car salesman here) to sell businesses and individuals on the benefits of banking with their institution

Commercial Banking Job Options

Credit Analyst

The credit analyst is the most widely held banking position. Credit analysts are responsible for evaluating personal and business loan applications. A strong understanding of business and corporate finance is important for predicting future cash flows and other factors that determine the credit quality of the client.

Loan Officer

A loan officer works directly with the consumer or business to approve or deny a loan. Loan officers should have strong communication skills, financial knowledge, and the determination to find new business loans for the bank.

Branch Manager

Branch managers are responsible for controlling all aspects of a retail bank branch. Their duties range from loan origination to managing deposits to daily customer service. Branch managers often start their careers as tellers or customer service repre-sentatives and eventually have the opportunity to manage an entire market or region.

Trust Officer

As a trust officer, individuals deliver trust services and financial advice to banking cus-tomers. These employees must be well versed in estate planning, taxes, probate law, and personal investing.

Mortgage Banker

A mortgage banker is responsible for originating and evaluating mortgage loans. They must be well versed in the principles of real estate, perform background and credit checks, and work closely with real estate agents. Strong analytical and people skills are necessary for success in this field.

Commercial banking provides the opportunity to combine sales, marketing, and fi-nancial expertise. If you enjoy working with people and selling a product or concept while still holding a financial position, commercial banking may be the perfect fit for you.

3. Investment Banking (IB)

The first thought that often comes to mind when people hear the words "investment bankers" are rich guys who work in New York City. A cloud of confusion generally sur-rounds IB, leaving students unsure about what investment bankers actually do. Simply put, investment bankers are responsible for helping businesses value (establish a sale price) and sell new stock (an ownership stake in the company) to investors.

Successful investment bankers have the following skills:

- Strong analytical and interpersonal skills
- Thinking outside the box
- The capability to handle high pressure situations and long work hours

Investment bankers typically start as junior analysts. Analysts serve as support for the senior investment bankers and, at times, work exhausting hours (eighty to one hundred hours per week). That being said, starting salaries (ranging from $60,000 to $120,000, plus bonuses) are some of the highest for those with an undergraduate degree. The investment banking profession doesn't put much weight on the work-life balance. Students should carefully evaluate this opportunity to determine if it is right for them.

Is the high pay worth the sacrifices you'll be forced to make? Only you can answer that question.

4. Consulting

Like IB, consulting may be a profession you've heard a lot about, but you may not know much about what this type of career entails.

As a consultant, you are employed by a firm (e.g., McKinsey or Deloitte) that hires out your services to other businesses (e.g., Procter & Gamble or Ford) to solve a specific problem within their company. Consulting firms charge the businesses per hour for your work, which can last anywhere from a couple weeks to several years. Generally, when working for one of the bigger consulting firms, employees follow a "four days out, one day in" schedule. This means you fly out Monday morning to your assignment (clients are often in another city), work there all week, fly back Thursday evening, and spend Friday in your firm's office to regroup and catch up. Consulting requires a lot of travel and the ability to work long hours, but it can be a very lucrative and rewarding profession.

The industry is very competitive and requires consultants to have the following skills:

- Very strong analytical skills—the job is to take information, synthesize it, and produce a viable solution.
- Great people skills and exceptional listening skills—consultants must conduct interviews with their clients to determine the root of the problem and then develop an effective solution.
- Be creative and possess a high level of mental horsepower—consultants are paid to provide valued advice and intelligence, and the ability to present solutions effectively is paramount.

Consulting careers typically begin in a position as a business analyst or junior analyst (different firms will use different terminology). McKinsey & Company, one of the top management consulting firms in the world, shows the following as a typical career path in consulting:

Business analyst -> graduate school -> associate -> engagement manager -> associate principal -> partner -> director[2]

Most prominent consulting firms want their employees to work for a few years to gain experience before sending them back to business school to get an MBA. The consulting profession is a high-risk, high-reward profession, with starting salaries at top firms exceeding $85,000 for business analysts. However, competition for the positions at these firms is very high, and the competitive nature of the job only increases after you're hired. Expect high-pressure situations, long hours, and a great deal of travel, while consistently demonstrating your value to the firm.

Finally, before interviewing for consulting positions, you should be familiar with the case-based interview method. Consulting firms conduct a different type of interview, one that requires an applicant to assess a problem, gather information, and provide a solution. After all, that's what you'll have to do if you land the job.

As we mentioned above, a finance degree provides graduates with a wide variety of opportunities, and our list is just the tip of the iceberg. No matter what your field of interest is, you would be best served to do some real research on your own to find a job that fits your skills, keeps you interested, and is something you can be excited about doing every day.

Careers in Economics

Fundamentally, the biggest difference between economics and finance/accounting is scale. Economics should be thought of as "the big picture" (how the market in a region or country is doing financially), while finance and accounting are generally more concerned with the well-being of a company or specific industry. There are a number of different types of economists, including, but not limited to, the following[3]:

- Microeconomists, who study individual people or businesses looking at supply and demand in an attempt to maximize production
- Macroeconomists, who focus on a broad-based economy, looking for trends in inflation, unemployment productivity, etc.
- Financial economists, who look at interest rates and their effects on the economy

---

2 http://www.mckinsey.com/careers/is_mckinsey_right_for_me/roles_and_career_paths.aspx

3 http://www.careeroverview.com/economist-careers.html

- International economists, who evaluate international markets, currency fluctuations, and the effects of foreign taxes and tariffs on goods and services
- Industrial economists, who study specific industries to help targeted businesses remain competitive
- Labor economists, who analyze trends in employee compensation, unemployment, and the effects of population shifts on a country's labor force
- Public finance economists, who focus on a government's involvement in the broad-based economy, looking specifically at budgeting and taxation
- Econometricians, who use mathematics, including calculus, regression analysis, and game theory, to build complex models to explain economic happenings and predict future outcomes

If you're serious about a career in economics, an advanced degree (MA, PhD) is usually a requirement for any kind of career advancement. As an economist, you generally work in either the public (government) or private sector. A 2006 study showed economists held approximately fifteen thousand jobs, and roughly 52 percent of them worked as government employees either at the state or federal level. Alternate career paths include working in the private sector as economic consultants, working in academia as a teacher or professor, or holding a coveted position in finance, marketing, and operations. According to a 2007 survey, economics majors ranked fifth in average starting salary among bachelor degree recipients—see the full list below.

Average Starting Salary—Bachelor Degree Recipients—2013-14[4]

1. Chemical Engineering—$68,200
2. Electrical Engineering—$64,300
3. Computer Science—$59,800
4. Civil Engineering—$54,300
5. Economics—$50,100
6. Finance—$49,200
7. Accounting—$45,300
8. Chemistry—$44,100
9. Business Administration/Management—$43,500
10. Marketing—$40,200

---

4 "2013-14 PayScale College Salary Report" www.payscale.com/college-salary-report-2014/majors-that-pay-you-back.

Thinking about Law School?

Interpreting contracts, facilitating mergers and acquisitions, and being familiar with local, state, and federal tax codes all have significant economic applications and are all useful skills for an aspiring attorney. According to the *Journal of Economic Education,* economics majors had the highest average LSAT score by major.

Average LSAT Scores by Major[5]:

1. Economics—156.6
2. Engineering—155.4
3. History—155.0
4. English—154.3
5. Finance—152.6
6. Political science—152.1
7. Psychology—152.1
8. Criminal justice—144.7

*Average score—152.2

An economics degree can be a great springboard for admission to a prestigious graduate program and lay a solid foundation for a career in consulting, public service, or academia. As always, do your best to define your personal goals and career aspirations, and then ask yourself whether a degree in economics is best suited to help you achieve those goals.

Careers in Marketing

Finally, let's take a look at some career options available to those who have a marketing degree. Marketing entails the activities necessary to transfer a product or service from the producer/seller to the end consumer. In an attempt to give a broad overview of the marketing world, we will touch on the following marketing segments:

1. Advertising and public relations
2. Market research
3. Product/brand management

---

5   Michael Nieswiadomy, "LSAT Scores of Economics Majors: The 2003–04 Class Update," *Journal of Economic Education* 37 #2, Spring 2006. Pp. 244–7. Available in JSTOR.

Advertising and Public Relations (PR)

It's safe to say most people have a high-level understanding of advertising and its importance in the marketing of products and services. In today's fast-paced, consumer-driven society, the average person is exposed to an estimated 280 advertisements per day. Assuming you sleep eight hours per night, that's one ad every four minutes!

With so much overexposure, advertising professionals are forced to evolve their methods of targeting consumers. We are immersed in an ad revolution. Marketers are moving from print and television mediums to digital outlets such as phones, tablets, social media, and even smart watches. Advertising firms and agencies are forced to be innovative in the development and delivery of their ads; their employees must be creative professionals who bring a fresh approach and can deliver results for their clients.

A successful advertising professional has the following skill set:

- The ability to work under pressure and meet critical deadlines for projects and campaigns
- A high level of creativity
- Knowledge of evolving industry trends
- The ability to think and work globally
- The ability to work well with other people and employ extraordinary communication skills

Advertising and public relations offer several job options...

Media Planner

Media planners decide how an advertisement and marketing message will be delivered to the public. They determine the right mix of different medias such as television, print, radio, desktop, and mobile devices, to name a few.

Copywriter/Illustrator

Copywriters and illustrators are responsible for the creative services surrounding the development of an advertisement. Job responsibilities include writing ad copy (the words used in the advertisement) and designing the advertisement and message.

Production Manager
Production managers are in charge of how the company promotes itself to the public or its customers. That is how ads are presented in print, in television, on radio, on billboards, or online.

Director of Advertising and Promotions
Directors are in charge of coordinating entire advertising campaigns—including project acquisition, budgeting, planning, and production.

Public Relations Specialist
A PR specialist manages the public view of a business or organization. The individual must be responsible for reading the public and reacting to its view of the company. The specialist is responsible for delivering messages and programs that promote a positive image for the organization.

Account Executive
An account executive is in charge of managing all services for a particular client or a number of clients of the firm. This includes ad campaigns, planning, implementation, and customer service.

In reading this section, you may have discerned that a career in advertising and PR is not for the faint of heart. Advertising professionals are under constant pressure to meet deadlines and are consistently evolving to keep up with the ever-changing demands of the industry. Top positions are highly competitive, and candidates must be willing to work hard and pay their dues to have the opportunity to fill these coveted roles. Be sure to do your due diligence and research whether or not this career path is the right fit for your talents and passions. This is a career that will absolutely keep you interested and on your toes.

Market Research
As you walk down the cereal aisle, have you ever wondered why people pick Fruit Loops or Fruity Pebbles, Lucky Charms or Cinnamon Toast Crunch? Or, in the detergent aisle, why a consumer chooses All rather than Tide, or Cheer rather than Gain?

Why does a person buy a BMW rather than a Mercedes or get his or her burger from McDonald's rather than Wendy's? These questions are the essence of what we call market research—understanding the consumer, why he or she behaves a certain way, and what positively or negatively affects his or her buying decisions.

Market research professionals seek to uncover this information through various research techniques such as surveys, interviews, focus groups (getting a group of people together to talk about predetermined topics), shop-alongs (watching the consumer shop and observing his or her buying habits), and consumer feedback. The researcher compiles the results of the research, analyzes the data, draws conclusions, and makes recommendations to the business. These recommendations help the business determine how to improve sales, gain market share, or increase awareness of its product or service.

Market research professionals have the following skills:

- The ability to collect and synthesize large amounts of data
- Extremely strong analytical skills
- Creativity in developing new ways to collect data
- The ability to use the results of their studies to develop solutions for company problems
- The knowledge to use both qualitative (nonnumerical) and quantitative (numerical) data to reach a conclusion

Upon entering the workforce, market research analysts can be employed directly by a company or work independently as a consultant. These professionals must think globally, understand consumer behavior, and be able to identify market trends. Market research positions often require a master's degree or doctorate; however, they are generally well compensated, with average salaries for MBA students ranging from $80,000 to $105,000.

Product and Brand Management

In the previous section, we discussed the job responsibilities of the market research professional and the importance of collecting and analyzing data in an effort to deliver recommendations on how to improve certain products and services. The image and value of a brand is very important to a business. According to BrandZ's 2014 report, the brand value of Coca-Cola is over $80 billion, and Google's brand is valued at nearly

$160 billion. Estimating all the future earnings of a firm and then discounting them back to present day levels provides the derivation of brand value. If you are confused by the terms "discounting" and "present day," Google "time value of money," as this is a very important concept in business.

Brands and brand value explain why we are brand loyal to certain products. For companies like Nike, McDonald's, IBM, and Apple, brand value is of utmost importance and is dynamic in nature. Consequently, it is the job of the brand manager to strategically position the brand to gain value.

A brand manager holds one of the most highly coveted positions in marketing and must have the following skill set:

- The ability to create change and control the image of a product or brand
- The ability to think globally and understand the consumer
- Strong analytical skills and the capability of developing strategic initiatives to strengthen a brand
- Exceptional communication skills and the ability to implement his or her strategies

One of the biggest decisions for graduates who want to become brand managers is to determine which industry and product/service group they have an interest in. Are you tech savvy? If so, you might enjoy managing a new line of computers for Dell. Or do you see yourself managing the rollout of a new line of athletic wear at Nike? These are important considerations as you determine if a job in brand management is right for you.

Just Getting Started

While this section was long, it presented only the tip of the iceberg in terms of job and career options for those with a business degree. The goal of this section was to provide you with a broad-based overview of different jobs in accounting, finance, economics, and marketing to help you understand the different segments of each function.

Deciding what to study in school may seem like a huge decision, and it is definitely an important one. But the first step in making an informed decision is getting to know the options each major will afford you upon graduation. Understanding and loosely defining your goals can help you make the right decision early on. Further research on areas in which you have the most interest will help identify what career you would enjoy.

This isn't rocket science. If you enjoy what you learn about a career, and the job sounds appealing, chances are you'll be happy doing it daily. Finally, remember that you, and you alone, can make the final decision. It is *your* life. Listen to the advice of family and friends, but don't become a doctor or an economist simply because it's what Mom or Dad wants. Do your homework. Research your options. Make an informed decision. And think "empowerment," not "imprisonment."

One final piece of advice before we talk about the most effective ways to get involved on campus. Your reputation as a student, a professional, and most importantly as a person, is something that takes years to build and seconds to destroy. Even if you have the grades to land your dream job or a top five MBA program acceptance letter, a glaring black spot on your resume can kill your chances before you get started.

The following is a note on integrity by Jack Lindquist. Jack an undergraduate business, James Scholar Honor Student, and the course manager for Business 101 at the University of Illinois at Urbana-Champaign.

As we enter the next chapter of our lives, we get a fresh start in many ways. We have the opportunity to become whoever we want to be and do whatever we want to do. And in four short years we'll walk out of here with an undergraduate degree, start another new chapter, and face a new set of challenges. But one thing that will follow us wherever we go is our reputation.

As college students, academic integrity is an essential component of our reputation. Conducting ourselves responsibly and holding ourselves accountable for all of our actions is an expectation that our peers, our professors, and our administrators hold for us. This encompasses everything from showing up for class on time to making the tough, ethical decisions. This definitely isn't high school anymore!

You may be wondering: what's the big deal? So what if I didn't properly cite my source in an essay for some Gen-Ed English class? Why does my university seem so concerned about my online source for an assignment? Why does letting my friend borrow some of my work lead to an uncomfortable meeting with the Dean of Students? Inflating your GPA by a few points or putting false information on your resume to land your dream internship is easy to rationalize for some, but these ethical decisions and questions of character can have serious implications down the line.

Integrity is crucial in college because you're developing skills that translate into a lifetime of good habits and behaviors that will affect you and everyone around you. When you don't properly cite your sources for an essay, you fail to give credit to somebody else's original thoughts. That's theft. When you use a web site's information without verifying the source, you could be misleading and even endangering people in the process. Letting someone copy your assignment seems like you're helping out a friend, but your friend is really losing out because they didn't learn that information. If they end up in a job they aren't qualified for, there is sure to be negative consequences. And giving false information on a resume misrepresents you, your skillsets, and starts a series of lies that can snowball out of control.

It's up to us, the leaders of tomorrow, to create a strong reputation for our generation. Act with integrity, don't be afraid to stand up for what you believe in, and remember that your actions can have an impact on the rest of society. Take charge of your environment and create the change that you'd like to see.

You may be thinking to yourself, "Hold on, Jack. I'm just starting college and you're already plotting how I'm going to change the world?" Yes! We're in business school because we want to make a difference for the people in our lives and the world. Our society is filled with examples of college students becoming founders of Fortune 500 companies from their dorm rooms. The ethical challenges they faced are not so different than the ones you will face in the coming years.

Start your college career by building a reputation you're proud of, one that will help you achieve your dreams and positively impact others in the process. It starts with us, but by no means will it end there!

CHAPTER 2

Getting Involved on Campus

As we mentioned in the foreword, the goal of this book is to help you be competitive when applying for top internships and job opportunities upon graduation by covering topics you might not learn in the classroom. We don't want you to just *survive*; we want you to *thrive* among your peers.

So far we have navigated through the crucial decisions of school and major selection. Now let's dive into some important differences between high school and college extracurricular involvement.

High School vs. College Academics

If you're reading this as a first-semester freshman, you're probably getting settled into your new academic routine—one that's far different from the set, five-days-a-week, 8:00 a.m. to 3:00 p.m. schedule you followed in high school. College life might appear easier and more laid-back, filled with opportunities to party, sleep until noon, and go weeks without homework, but we'd like to extend a word of caution—college is *not* the same as high school.

Yes, you may be able to schedule all your classes in the afternoon or have no classes on Friday, but don't be fooled into thinking it's going to be a cakewalk. University-level education places more responsibility on the student to learn autonomously. In high school, studying meant cramming and memorizing the night before for the next day's test. In college, studying that way is a first-class ticket to failing. Studying should be a daily habit of reading, doing assigned problems, and learning the material a little bit at a time.

Depending on the course, exams may happen only a few times a semester, cover a lot of material, and be worth 40 to 50 percent of your grade. Is it realistic to expect every college student to head straight from class to a two-hour study session in the library? Of course not. But staying on top of your studies by doing a little bit of work each day will greatly lower the level of stress you will feel when the first set of exams rolls around. And, by the way, all those exams will inevitably be scheduled during the same week. The pressure to do well academically can be overwhelming for first-year students. But, if you are disciplined and make it a point to layer the material instead of cramming at the end, the grades you want will follow in due course.

Finally, here are a few reminders and thoughts on university academics:

- Work with your friends. They can be excellent study partners and they usually make studying more tolerable.
- Chances are you probably will get a bad grade on something in your first semester. Don't stress out. It may require a little extra work, but learn from your mistakes, and do better next time.
- Don't stumble in the starting blocks. It's hard to win the race (graduate with the grades you want) if you get off to a slow start.
- Get to know your teachers. College courses can have 150 to 300 students in one class. A personal relationship with your teacher can really help you to do well; arriving early to class is a good starting point.
- Success in college is not solely tied to your academic performance. Find a club, team, or group to get involved in. This will help you set yourself apart from your peers.

The Fun Part of College—Getting Involved on Campus!

I know, I know. You probably just rolled your eyes, but wait. Getting involved really can be an awesome experience.

Most schools, especially larger universities, offer a variety of student-run clubs and organizations. Involvement in something outside of the classroom or visiting your favorite bar can bring great balance to your life and provide invaluable experiences. By the time you're done with college, you'll understand why your parents said they learned more in college outside of the classroom than in it.

Getting involved on campus is essential for a variety of reasons:

1. Networking. Your network could prove to be your single greatest asset after you graduate.
2. Clubs and organizations allow you to get experience in areas that you are passionate about.
3. Involvement in a club, group, or team will give you experiences to talk about during interviews.
4. Any leadership experience on your résumé will give you a decided advantage over your future competition. Hold a leadership position in the organization, improve your communication skills, and add another positive checkmark on your résumé.

The three most important skills companies look for in undergraduate candidates are as follows:

1. Leadership experience
2. Strong academics
3. Great communication skills

Two-thirds of these can be developed through campus involvement.

Depth, Not Breadth

As you explore different opportunities to get involved, forget the high school mentality of participating in as many clubs/groups/teams as you can. Extracurricular involvement in college is different; the number of organizations is not nearly as important as your level of involvement.

Did you hold a leadership position? How were you involved? Did you start any new events or traditions? These are questions interviewers will ask. Seasoned recruiters will see right through the ploy of students who sign up for every organization simply to build a résumé.

Finally, while it's important to gain experience and have valuable material for an interview, these should not be the driving factors for your involvement. You have a finite amount of time in college. Make the best of it, and truly enjoy the clubs and teams in which you are involved!

Twenty-One Ways to Get Involved!

Finding a balance between academics and extracurricular activities is extremely important. Students often put too much emphasis on one or the other, but recruiters look for a combination of a strong academics and leadership skills. Keep in mind that you are a student first. When responsibilities begin to mount, school should be your top priority.

Finally, we'd like to make a small disclaimer. The following suggestions are just a sample of the opportunities available to students. It's been harped on almost *ad nauseam*, but individual research and having a good understanding of all your options is very important. Seek out unique opportunities on your campus by attending organizational fairs and talking to other students.

Without further ado, here are twenty-one ways to get involved (in no particular order):

1. **Join a business/professional fraternity.**

    Professional business fraternities structure their organizations like actual businesses, with elected leadership positions such as president, vice president of marketing, vice president of finance, and director of human resources. Involvement provides members with valuable experience in a variety of business functions. In some chapters, members have the opportunity to work on projects with external clients as well as participate in various other forms of professional programming, including résumé workshops, interview training, and presentation workshops.

    Three well-known national business fraternities that may have chapters on your campus are as follows:

    -   Pi Sigma Epsilon (www.pse.org) specializes in developing marketing and sales professionals through lifetime opportunities. Founded in 1951, it has 132 chapters.[6]
    -   Delta Sigma Pi (www.dspnet.org) specializes in fostering the study of business in universities. It encourages scholarship, social activity, and the association of students for their mutual advancement. Founded in 1907, it has 260 chapters.[7]

---

6 www.pse.org

7 www.dspnet.org

- Alpha Kappa Psi (www.akpsi.org) was founded on the principles of educating its members and the public to appreciate and demand higher ideals in business and to promote the individual welfare of members during college and beyond. Founded in 1904, it has more than 300 chapters.[8]

2. **Join a social fraternity or sorority.**

   This is what most people think of when hearing about "frats and sororities." Depending on the school, there may be dozens of houses to pick from, which can make finding the right one difficult. If you find yourself in this situation, do some research. Talk to older friends who are both Greek and non-Greek to gain perspective, and "rush" several houses to determine whether or not a particular house fits your personality.

   Deciding whether or not to rush can be a big decision. Sometimes freshman get caught up in the excitement of the Greek system and feel like they have to get involved with a fraternity or sorority to meet new people. Fraternities and sororities can be beneficial for some students, but they aren't for everyone, and membership comes at a price.

   Some benefits of joining a fraternity or sorority include the following[9]:

   - Brotherhood and sisterhood. The opportunity to meet a lot of people and develop lifelong friendships.
   - Academics. One goal of the Greek community is to encourage and promote high levels of academic achievement through peer tutoring, group studying, and counseling by older members.
   - Leadership. Numerous opportunities exist for leadership development ranging from leading/taking charge of an event/duty to holding a nominated or elected position within the chapter.
   - Community service. Fraternities and sororities place a strong emphasis on giving back to local communities and causes through community service events and initiatives. It is estimated that the Greek community donates over ten million hours of service annually.
   - Career networking. Upon graduation, being a member will provide you with a great network to seek out opportunities for jobs and postgraduate studies.

---

8 www.akpsi.org

9 http://www.greeks.psu.edu/benefits.htm

Like every decision, pros and cons exist. It is up to you to do the necessary research to determine if Greek life is right for you.

3. **Join a service fraternity.**

If you read through the first two suggestions and neither sounded interesting, a third type of fraternity (not as well known) is a service fraternity. Service frats are just what their name implies: they are organized campus-run groups focused on community service efforts. By joining a service fraternity, students have the opportunity to develop as leaders while giving back their time and talents.

Alpha Phi Omega is an example of a well-known national service fraternity, with more than seventeen thousand members at 366 campuses nationwide. Their mission is "to prepare campus and community leaders through service," and their overall purpose is to "develop leadership, to promote friendship, and to provide service to humanity."[10]

With a large national membership and chapters across the country, a membership in a service fraternity can provide you with unparalleled leadership experience and a well-connected network upon graduation.

4. **Run for student government.**

Are you interested in the exciting, ever-changing world of politics? Does running for public office sound appealing to you? The chance to work with your local representative on a meaningful campaign is an invaluable experience. Any and all of these reasons can be motivation enough to run for a position in your university's student government. This type of position can provide you with great leadership experience, the opportunity to network within a field of interest, and the help you need to develop strong communication skills.

5. **Become an RA (residence advisor).**

Residence hall advisors, or assistants, are trained peer leaders who supervise students living in a residence hall. RAs are typically second-, third-, or fourth-year students, who have responsibilities and benefits, including the following:
- Access to free on-campus housing and meal plans

---

10 http://www.apo.org/pages/show/About_Us

- Privilege of acting as first resource with academic or institutional questions
- Chance to develop personal skills as a mediator, problem solver and a mentor for younger men and women
- Opportunity to gain leadership experience through the development of meaningful programming for residents

If you are interested in becoming an RA, be ready for some competition. These are generally sought-after positions and involve a multistep interview process. Be sure to review the university's website for more information regarding requirements and deadlines for application. If you plan to be an RA, it's best to start the application process a year earlier.

6. **Get involved with a local church/synagogue/mosque.**

Becoming a member of a local church, synagogue, or mosque is a great way to meet like-minded people within the student community and surrounding communities while practicing something you're passionate about. Weekly services, retreats, prayer groups, or community-related events are some ways to get involved and display your leadership skills.

7. **Get an on-campus job.**

Earn a couple extra dollars and demonstrate your ability to balance work, school, and a social life by taking an on-campus job. If this is something you're interested in, staying with the same employer throughout college is beneficial for a number of reasons. Once again, it may afford you the opportunity to be promoted to a leadership position. Advancing to the management level shows potential employers you are willing and capable of remaining committed to a team or a company.

8. **Join a club sports team.**

If you are like most high school athletes, you probably enjoyed your time in high school sports but decided to hang up your cleats before college. If so, trying out for a club sports team may be a nice compromise. Most university club sports teams are highly selective and will compete against teams from other universities. If you don't make the cut, don't be discouraged. If it's something you want to do for fun, there are plenty of opportunities to play intramural sports, which are more relaxing and require less of a time commitment.

9. **Join the school band.**

   Joining the school band may require some prior musical talent, but doing so is another way to develop your skills while meeting new people and becoming part of the campus community. *How* you choose to get involved is less important than actually *getting* involved. For some students this is very easy and comes almost naturally; others may need to push themselves to become involved. While it might seem a little bit uncomfortable at first, I assure you it will become easier as you become better acclimated with campus life.

10. **Try out for a part in a university play or musical.**

    The ability to deliver a sharp, effective presentation and be comfortable speaking in front of a large group of people will pay dividends in the business world. Acting in a university production is a great way to not only meet people but also develop your communication and presentation skills. Often, young business professionals are behind the curve when it comes to presenting (a skill that can only be developed through practice) and overall communication. In gaining valuable acting experience during college, you get a leg up on the competition.

11. **Join College Democrats or College Republicans.**

    If you are interested in politics and discussing relevant issues but are not cut out for an elected office (see point four, "Run for student government"), joining College Democrats or College Republicans could be a great way to get involved. Membership in either organization would provide you with relevant exposure to political issues. Both College Republicans and College Democrats are very large national organizations with a presence on most university or college campus. Below is a little bit of information on each organization.

    College Republicans[11]

---

11 http://collegerepublicans.org/about

College Republicans is the nation's oldest, largest, and most active youth political organization. Founded in 1892, there are currently over two hundred thousand College Republicans around the country on more than eighteen hundred campuses in every state and in the District of Columbia.

Every year, College Republicans from all across America come together to help elect Republican candidates, support the Republican agenda, and become the future leaders of the conservative movement. College Republicans are the grassroots arm of the Republican Party, the counterbalance to unions and leftist interest groups.

College Democrats[12]
College Democrats is a political organization representing the other side of the aisle. Every year, College Democrats from all across the nation come together to help elect Democratic candidates, support the more liberal, Democratic agenda, and become future leaders in the Democratic Party.

12. Join a club centered on your field of study.
There are a variety of clubs and teams tailored to provide experience for a particular major or field of study.
- Student investment group
- Accounting or marketing-based case study competitions
- Student-run venture funds (These decide how to allocate and investment capital in start-up businesses developed by university students.)
- Zoology club
- Prelaw club
- Premedicine club
- Predental club

Many of these clubs provide experience specific to an industry. Take a venture capital club, for example. Working with a VC club can give you true insight into a given industry, providing perspective on whether or not you can see yourself pursuing work in that industry as a career.

---

12 http://www.collegedems.com/issues.html

13. **Pursue academic research with a university professor.**

    Think about your favorite professors from the past few semesters. Chances are at least one of these men or women are teaching in a field that interests you. Partnering with a university professor to conduct academic research is a terrific way to learn more about a field of interest and add a credible reference to your résumé.

    These opportunities may not be highly publicized on campus, but that doesn't mean they don't exist. Be proactive. Seek out the opportunity. This is a microcosm of the work world. People who take the extra step are people who find themselves at the top of their profession.

14. **Join a campus a cappella/glee club/choir/opera group.**

    You'll need some musical background or vocal talent to join one of these groups, but the experience can be very rewarding. College a cappella groups are becoming increasingly more popular (no really, they are!).

    Did you know a cappella–style music was first created in a New Haven bar in 1909? A group known as the Yale Whiffenpoofs sang (slightly inebriated) without music at a bar, and thus the first campus a cappella group was created. Over the last hundred years, over twelve hundred groups have been formed at colleges and universities across the United States (told ya).

15. **Join the campus mock-trial team.**

    If you're interested in becoming the next Atticus Finch, mock trials can help your practical litigation experience by giving you the opportunity of going head to head against colleges and universities in mock trial competitions. Interested in law and business? Keep the JD/MBA degree on your radar; this program is a lot of work—in general, completing both degrees takes three years—but it will make you extremely marketable upon graduation.

16. **Get involved with the campus radio station/TV station.**

    If you read chapter two and thought, "Hey, PR sounds pretty sweet!" you might find that doing some work with the campus radio or TV station can be very valuable experience. Hosting your own show, while learning the business side of the production, will put you ahead of the game when you graduate.

17. Apply for a sports-marketing position with the campus athletic department.

The business of sports is as competitive as any industry out there. Thousands of graduates apply for a limited number of available positions in the world of sports. That being said, experience in sports marketing before you graduate can set you apart. These positions generally function as a semester or yearlong (sometimes paid) internship. The perks that come with this type of position are endless: good seats for or field access to all university sporting events, the opportunity to gain valuable marketing experience, and extra spending money—just to name a few. Be sure to seek this type of position early; they're highly competitive and often involve a series of interviews.

18. Join a cultural club or student organization.

Students often join a cultural club to meet students from a similar background and find a sense of belonging. However, joining a club (one that isn't your culture) is a great way to learn more about different types of people and broaden your horizons.

19. Join a student organization supporting a cause or belief.

Are you passionate about a certain cause or belief? If you're at a large university, chances are good a group exists that either directly or indirectly supports this cause. If not, you can be the founder! For example, many service fraternities participate in a wide range of service-related activities (e.g., Habitat for Humanity, Relay For Life), and local religious communities organize everything from weekly trips to work in a local soup kitchen to week-long mission trips in impoverished regions around the globe.

20. Work for the university's newspaper or another on-campus publication.

In the ever-changing digital world, having an understanding of how media outlets function is a great asset. Much like the prominent earned media outlets, university papers generate revenue through advertising. By working at your university paper, you can acquire knowledge about the ad world—a world that is prevalent across almost all aspects of business.

21. **Become a tutor.**

   Whether they'll admit it or not, many students struggle academically during their freshman year. Did you take advantage of your school's tutoring services? If you benefitted from knowing a great tutor, think about giving back by being one yourself. This can be a rewarding experience, as you learn to teach and help other students understand difficult concepts.

A Quick Review

So there you have them—twenty-one ways to get involved on your college campus. While selecting a club or group that gives you major-related experience is beneficial, it is more important to join a group that represents something you are truly passionate about. As a student, it is less important *what* you do and more important *that* you do something.

Finally, remember that college is different from high school. Deep involvement in one or two organizations is much more important than a nominal membership in five or six.

Be proactive. Seek out unique opportunities on campus that will not only give you great experience but also afford you the opportunity to meet new friends, build a young professional network, and have a great time in the process.

CHAPTER 3

Becoming an Excellent Communicator

As you begin looking for internships or full-time employment, you'll notice a few recurring characteristics that recruiters are looking for in potential hires, such as leadership skills, strong academic record, and exceptional communication skills.

In this chapter we focus on the latter. Your ability to present an idea in a confident and succinct manner is paramount for success in the business world.

Let's Turn to the Experts

Part One: The Exceptional Presenter

Tim Koegel, author of *The Exceptional Presenter: A Proven Formula to Open Up! and Own the Room* was kind enough to write this chapter. Tim works with executives, politicians, and business professionals to craft their message and refine their delivery skills. As a presentation and media consultant, Tim has strengthened the presentations, media relations, and general communication skills of CEOs, world leaders, business executives, and sales professionals from Deloitte, Harvard Business School, GlaxoSmithKline, Cisco Systems, and the White House, just to name a few.

A graduate of the University of Notre Dame, Tim is also the author of *The Exceptional Presenter: The Definitive Handbook for Showcasing Your Message*[13].

The Exceptional Presenter

Becoming an exceptional presenter seems to be a Herculean task. There's a lot to remember. Say this. Move that. Speak up. Look at the audience. Don't fidget. There are a lot of "experts" out there who will give you all the answers. Type the words "public speaking" into a leading Internet search engine, and you'll get 84,300,000 listings. It can be overwhelming. After a while, it all seems to sound the same. The formula you are about to learn will take the mystery and the misery out of presenting. We will break down the art of presenting into a series of skills. Then you will learn a systematic approach to mastering each skill.

Open Up!

OPEN UP! is an acronym representing the six characteristics shared by exceptional presenters. The secret is not just knowing the characteristics but understanding how to incorporate them into your presentation style.

The exceptional presenter is as follows:

Organized

Exceptional presenters take charge. They look poised and polished. They sound prepared. You get the sense that they are not there to waste time. Their goal is not to overwhelm, but to inform, persuade, influence, entertain, or enlighten. Their message is well structured and clearly defined.

Passionate

Exceptional presenters exude enthusiasm and conviction. If the presenter doesn't look, sound, and act passionate about his or her topic, why would anyone else be passionate about it? Exceptional presenters speak from the heart and leave no doubt as to where they stand. Their energy is persuasive and contagious.

---

13 http://www.presentationacademy.com/about-tim-koegel.cfm

Engaging

Exceptional presenters do everything in their power to engage each audience member. They build rapport quickly and involve the members of the audience early and often. If you want their respect, you first connect.

Natural

An exceptional presenter's style is natural. His or her delivery has a conversational feel. Natural presenters make it look easy. They appear comfortable with any audience. A presenter who appears natural appears confident.

As an exceptional presenter, you must keep the following in mind as you prepare:

Understand Your Audience

Exceptional presenters learn as much as they can about their audience before presenting to them. The more they know about the audience, the easier it will be to connect and engage.

Practice

Those who practice improve. Those who don't, don't. Exceptional skills must become second nature. Practice is the most important part of the improvement process. If your delivery skills are second nature, they will not fail under pressure. There are hundreds of opportunities every day to practice the skills in this chapter. The only thing you need is the desire to practice. Most people never practice. If they do, it's on their way to present a proposal, interview for a job, deliver a keynote presentation, or sell an idea to their boss. The time to practice is not in live win-or-lose situations. The time to practice is during your normal daily routine, when habits can be formed and mistakes are not costly.

It's Not Where You Start; It's Where You Finish

There has never been a more important time to possess exceptional presentation skills. Every year the *Wall Street Journal* (*WSJ*) publishes its corporate recruiters survey. The survey ranks business schools based on the input it receives from corporate recruiters, the people who interview and hire MBA students. One part of the survey includes attributes recruiters list as "very important" for MBA job candidates. The hiring attribute consistently found at the top of the list is communication and interpersonal skills. People who possess exceptional communication skills maintain a distinct competitive advantage in winning new business and securing the best jobs. There are a few things to remember, however.

Do not discount your potential as a presenter. No matter what your skill level, no matter your presentation comfort level—you can become exceptional.

Do not underestimate the power of your delivery. Consider the results of Dr. Albert Mahrabian's study on what determines communication impact:

- Words we use—7 percent
- Our voice (confidence factor)—38 percent
- Nonverbal cues (posture, appearance, gestures, eye movement)—55 percent

Do not underestimate how often you use these skills. Every time you open your mouth to speak in public, you are a public speaker.

Organized: Structuring Your Story
Consider the following facts:

- Studies suggest the average adult's "undivided attention span" is fifteen to thirty seconds.
- Most people will forget 95 percent of what you say within minutes of hearing your message.

That being said...Keep it short...Keep in relevant...Keep it focused. Below is a simple structure to help you organized your presentations:

1. Begin with a purpose. Complete the following sentence: "If you remember just one thing as you leave here today, remember this..." By completing that sentence, you have successfully identified the most relevant information in your presentation. As you build your presentation, never lose sight of that one thing. It is your purpose. Remember, if you tell people what they are about to hear, they are more likely to hear it. Effective openings include a quote, a statistic, a question to the audience, a current event, a story, a sincere thank-you, a humorous story, a prediction, or an extended pause.

2. Objective/purpose/mission/goal. You have successfully identified the purpose. Now use your objective/purpose/mission/goal to identify what you will cover. In other words, what is your agenda? Don't go into detail at this point; give the audience a thirty-thousand-foot view of your presentation. If you can't clearly define your objective, then there probably isn't a compelling reason to do the presentation.

3. Position/situation/issues. Make sure to outline the issues, concerns, fears, expectations, successes, or obstacles as you understand them. At this point in your presentation, stop and ask your audience if anything has changed. Are there other issues that are relevant to the discussion?

4. End result/benefits/consequences. What are the benefits, ramifications, consequences, and implications of taking, or not taking, action?

5. Next step/action plan/timeline. What is the next step? What are the expectations? Where do we go from here? Use the next step as your call to action. It will help you prepare your audience for what you expect of them and what they can expect of you.

The Sixty/Twenty Rule

Arrive sixty minutes before you are scheduled to present. Use the first forty minutes to prepare the room, seating, notes, AV equipment, handouts, and props. The twenty minutes prior to your presentation are prime time for introductions, information gathering, and rapport building. Remember, the goal is to "own the room!" You are responsible for the success or failure of the session. When the audience arrives, turn your undivided attention to them—introduce audience members to one another—be a conversation starter.

The Passionate Presenter

Exceptional presenters radiate passion, conviction, and enthusiasm. If you don't look and sound passionate about your topic, why would your audience be passionate about your topic? Feeling passionate is one thing. Looking and sounding passionate is quite another. Your body language, facial expressions, movement, gestures, and voice are the implements that convert words into action and transform the printed text into emotion and enthusiasm.

The Power of Nonverbal Communication

Remember, your nonverbal messages will override anything you say. Here are five tips to appear relaxed, confident, and professional:

1. Stand tall—don't sway, rock shuffle, or lean.
2. Keep your head and eyes up. Connect with your audience.
3. Smile. A sincere smile warms up the coldest situations.
4. Never retreat.
5. Move with purpose, energy, and enthusiasm.

Engaging: To Earn Their Respect, You Must First Connect

Here are eleven ways exceptional presenters connect with their audience:

1. Speak to the interests of your audience. People don't care how much you know, until they know how much you care.
2. Use stories, examples, and anecdotes.
3. Eye contact is an essential engagement tool.
4. Don't waste time talking to inanimate objects.
5. Smile.
6. Use names early and often.
7. Get to your feet.
8. Use current events and periodicals—you will create the impression that your information is fresh and that you are on top of what is happening in the world.
9. Humor—there is nothing like humor to break down barriers, build rapport, and disarm opponents. "Laughter is the short distance between two people" (Victor Borge).
10. Read your audience.
11. Get your audience involved—"I hear and I forget. I see and I remember. I do and understand" (Chinese proverb).

Practice, Practice, Practice!

A big thanks to Tim Koegel for his contribution to *Little Fish, Big Ocean*. Hopefully, after reading this chapter, you realize the importance of strong communication skills. They may be the single most important asset in business.

As you move through college, take advantage of every opportunity to improve your presentation and communication skills. Tim asks you to remember three keys things from this chapter:

1. Do not accept average when you can be exceptional.
2. Every contact counts. Every interview counts. Every presentation counts.
3. Those who practice, improve. Those who don't, don't.

The above chapter was a compilation of selected excerpts from Tim Koegel's book, *The Exceptional Presenter: A Proven Formula to Open Up! and Own the Room.* I encourage you to pick up Tim's book—it is a quick, informative, and enjoyable read, complete with examples, preparation sheets, detailed instructions, and helpful guides that will undoubtedly set you on the path to becoming an exceptional presenter.

Part Two: Professional Communication

Part two of chapter on becoming an excellent communicator comes from Kelly Janssen, the Director of Undergraduate Admissions for the College of Business at the University of Illinois. Kelly Janssen has taught professional communication to more than 5,000 business students at the University of Illinois and has worked with executives at Deloitte, John Deere, Grant Thorton, State Farm, and Ernst & Young and several others to determine the soft skills employers are seeking from interns and new hires. With 17 years' experience in higher education and degrees in Communication Training, Kelly is an expert when it comes to communication skills.

The Art of Professional Communication

As an incoming college student, everything is new and exciting! Students are getting acquainted to their new homes and starting to gather the information needed for their next four years. As you try to determine what information is important, think of your mind is a toolbox. Every stored resource, or tool, can help along the way. There are endless tools to select from and your toolbox is only so big, so choose wisely!

One tool you'll need the moment you step on campus is the powerful skill of effective communication.

Communication may seem second nature by the time we graduate high school, but as we enter higher education and the professional ranks, we are all judged by our ability to communicate effectively. You are about to enter a world that brings an elevated standard of communication. The manner in which you interact with mentors, professors, or even an older peer (who may become a hiring manager at your dream job) can make all the difference. Text messages, emails, phone calls, in-class discussions, interviews, coffee dates, study groups, formal meetings, and countless others can be effective or ineffective methods of communication. The good news is, you get to make the choice!

Communicating in a professional manner will be a constant work in progress throughout college. So, how do you become an excellent communicator? The five "**Be**" skills found below are a great start!

These "**Be**" skills were created directly from research studies and discussions with partners, recruiters, and high-ranking executives at small and large organizations and businesses such as Ernst & Young, Deloitte, KPMG, Deere & Company, BMO Financial, Abbott Laboratories, PNC, Motorola, Merrill Lynch, Prudential, Google, State Farm, AllState, and Pricewaterhouse Coopers.

Don't just take my word for it; take theirs! These are the ways to "**Be**."

1. Be present.

Get exposure to your vocation's communication styles as early as possible. While your classes will provide a nice base, supplement your education with other credible outlets. Start listening to NPR (National Public Radio) and reading *FORTUNE* or the *Wall Street Journal*. Want to intern or work for a specific company? Visit the company web site and the read through the investor documents. Make personal connections with your college professors and career services advisors; they have terrific knowledge and perspective. Talk to recruiters. Learn the types of skills they look for in future interns and employees. Seek out classes or other opportunities that can help you improve. Think of professional communication like a new language: you have to immerse yourself in it to really understand it.

Keep your focus on the task at hand, one task at a time. Multi-tasking can be your enemy when it comes to being present. A recruiter once told me, "I would rather have a new hire that excels in one specific area and could use some work in others than someone who can accomplish things in every area, but does so mediocrely." A report published in *Forbes* magazine showed that 56% of almost 64,000 surveyed managers see recent grads lacking attention to details that are essential to their job.[14]

---

14 http://www.forbes.com/sites/karstenstrauss/2016/05/17/these-are-the-skills-bosses-say-new-

How can you stay focused? One way is to handwrite your notes from class time, conversations, or meeting minutes. Studies show that information is more effectively retained when it's handwritten and includes defined goals and objectives.[15] Laptops and other electronic devices can be helpful, but they also can be a diversion. Think about all of the texts and emails that can pop up in the middle of a lecture. I know I'd be distracted!

Remember to keep the phones and tablets on silent and out of sight during class, meetings, presentations, and face-to-face interactions unless there is a specific purpose to have them out. Try to resist the urge to check your phone every two minutes. I know, it's hard! But keep in mind the impression you're making on the person you're talking to when you're constantly checking your phone. Keep the focus on the information being shared in that moment.

Actively listen. Don't just hear information, but take time to understand the points being made. Ask questions as you need, especially as it pertains to following directions and identifying potential roadblocks. Give your full attention to what others are saying and be open to reading verbal and non-verbal communication skills.

Active listening is essential to your success as a professional communicator and has a direct link to job performance. Studies show active listening is the most coveted skill of a business employee, beating out skills such as conflict management, persuasion, and negotiation. [16]

It takes time to and effort to practice active listening inside and outside the classroom. Often, once we have a formulated response or a preconceived notion, we'll tune out, waiting for our turn to share. Try not to do this! Be present and engaged as much as possible. Listen first and ask questions second. Remember, you have two ears and one mouth for a reason. No one likes to repeat themselves, especially professors and employers.

2. Be considerate of time and effort involved.

It's happened to all of us. Our phone rings and it's from an anonymous, unknown number. Do you pick up? Some people do, but others let it go to voicemail. In the meantime, you're wondering, *who's contacting me, what do they want, and why are they calling?*

college-grads-do-not-have/#7033a488596e

15 http://www.npr.org/2016/04/17/474525392/attention-students-put-your-laptops-away

16 Abstract found at http://amle.aom.org/content/14/2/205.abstract

Take that same concept and apply it to a professional communication situation. Consider the person on the other end and, prior to contact, think about:

- What information do I want or need to share or receive?
- What information will the other person need to help me accomplish my goal?
- If I were the other person, would I want to discuss this information via email? Text message? Phone call? In-person meeting? Formal presentation? Essentially, what is the most appropriate platform for communication?
- How urgent is the relaying of this information? Can it go on the back-burner or is this a fire that needs to be put out quickly? According to one firm partner, there is an enormous "lack of just picking up the phone and calling. We rely way too much on email when, in some cases, a phone call can address a question or concern immediately."
- What time commitment are you looking for from the other person? Every person's time is valuable, and it's important to respect that. One goal that a CFO shared for his employees: "Be concise in appointments/meetings: schedule for 30 minutes instead of 60, or better yet, 15-20 if possible."

Keep communication succinct and to the point. "Interns and new hires need to understand that leaders in the company are bombarded with information and don't have time to try to interpret information all the time; they need concise, fact-based recommendations for them to evaluate and make decisions." – Vice President of a prominent financial services firm.

3. Be overly and overtly respectful to everyone.

Unless you are casual friends, don't address professors, managers, or other higher-level individuals by their first name or a shortened version of their name until explicitly told you can do so. It's an easy way to show respect for a person's title and life position.

Choose your communication medium carefully, based on your audience. From a corporate partner: "IM is a huge pet peeve of mine in certain circumstances. I've had people I have never met send me an IM/email with no introduction, just a 'can you help me with...' question as the opener. Drives me crazy! Makes me feel like they view their question as more important than introducing themselves or whatever else I may be working on at the time. Honestly, I usually ignore them for a while before responding."

Stick with proper grammar and punctuation, and PROOFREAD. In the words of one VP: "Making up abbreviations and shortening up phrases into texting language doesn't work in the current work world. Today's students should understand there is a difference in what is communicated via texts & IMs, and what is in emails. Even though it's not as formal as a memo or report, grammar and punctuation are still important in email communication. Email is an extremely important tool for us and becoming even more important with things like virtual and global working relationships."

4. Be independent and comfortable with ambiguity.

Ambiguity introduces you to thinking on your own, recognizing problems and creating solutions. How does this tie in with professional communication?

Companies don't want robots. They want employees who can make independent decisions for both short-term and long-term projects. Sixty percent of those 63,924 survey managers said new graduates need increased critical thinking and problem solving skills.[17] Instead of requesting information down to every exact detail, challenge yourself to think on your own.

Independent thinking and results will set you apart in any profession you choose, but try not to jump at the first opportunity just to get something done. Take time to consider the possibilities and pursue the one(s) that resonate most. If you don't succeed, it's okay. You tried something new and demonstrated innovation and thoughtfulness instead of just providing canned responses. College is a place for you to nurture and grow confident in your abilities.

5. Be honest.

You screwed up. You forgot to submit an assignment, will be late to a meeting, or told someone incorrect information. Options: hide the issue (bad idea #1), blame someone or something else for the issue (bad idea #2), or directly address the issue,

---

17 http://www.forbes.com/sites/karstenstrauss/2016/05/17/these-are-the-skills-bosses-say-new-college-grads-do-not-have/#7033a488596e

accept personal responsibility, and determine the best course of action (winner-winner!). Figure out the best communication method (see #2), and then:

- Apologize if appropriate and acknowledge the issue.
- Discuss the situation and where things stand.
- Propose a revised plan of action.

This is probably the hardest of the **"Be"** skills to initially follow because no one ever wants to admit and face mistakes. The truth is, errors occur. The most important aspect of recovering from these errors is to show respect to the people affected through direct honesty. Those people may be upset about the error, but they will appreciate your truthfulness and willingness to make it right if possible. The more you practice personal accountability, the more it will feel like the natural response to issues you encounter. And the best place to mess up and learn from your mistakes? College.

And there you have it! Keep the five **"Be"** principles in your communication skills toolbox. They will serve you well throughout your college career and beyond. Raise the bar for yourself. See excellent communication practice as a requirement, not a recommended goal. It takes 30 days to form a habit. So, make it a daily practice to communicate well or don't communicate at all!

Quick story. I host workshops for talented high school juniors and seniors from around the country. One student left a lasting impression because of a perfectly crafted email he sent. The note was polite, professional, succinct, and contained a well thought-out question. Of the hundreds of students I've interacted with through workshops, he still stands out. If he were to contact me tomorrow and ask for a reference letter, I wouldn't hesitate to say yes. In a world that often lacks professional communication, that's how impressionable his actions were.

What kind of mark do you want to leave?

CHAPTER 4

Principles of Extraordinary Leadership

I n a world overly focused on personal advancement, we often forget that leadership is about developing those around you. By facilitating the success of others, you are helping grow an organization and cultivating your leadership skills in the process.

Becoming a great leader is not something that happens overnight. Leadership skills are mastered over time through continued learning, observation, and experience. In this chapter, Bob McDonald will explain what he believes makes a quality leader, and more importantly, a great person.

Bob McDonald—US Secretary of Veteran Affairs, retired chairman, president, and CEO of Proctor & Gamble

What I Believe in

By Robert (Bob) A. McDonald

Throughout my education, military, and business careers, there are a few principles in which I believe deeply that drive my behavior every day.

Book references:
Leader's Compass by Dennis Haley and Ed Ruggero
The Leadership Engine by Noel Tichy

1. **Living a life driven by purpose is more meaningful and rewarding than meandering through life without direction.** My life's purpose is to improve lives. This operates on many levels. I work to improve the lives of the seven billion people in the world with P&G brands, and I work every day to have a positive impact in the life of just one person. This life goal led me to be a Boy Scout when I was young, to attend West Point and become an officer in the US Army, and to join the Procter & Gamble Company. People like to work for leaders who operate with a clear and consistent purpose. The leader's job is to understand and enable the purpose and dreams of his or her employees. In this sense, the task of the leader becomes a calling, a profession, not a job.

Book Reference:
Man's Search for Meaning by Viktor Frankl

2. **Everyone wants to succeed, and success is contagious.** I have never in all my life, in any career, in any country, at any time, met a person who tries to fail. Everyone I have met wants to succeed. So the job of the leader is to help people succeed. A leader's job is to catch people succeeding, even if the success is a small one, and to use that small success to build a virtuous cycle of ever-larger successes. Since success is contagious, one success will always lead to another, and one successful person will always influence another to be successful. Our job as leaders is to start the fire that fuels the virtuous cycle of success.

Book reference:
The Dream Manager by Michael Kelly

3. **Putting people in the right jobs is one of the most important jobs of the leader.** People like to do work that they are good at. Think about your education. What was your favorite class? What was your grade in that class? Chances are the class you liked the most was also the one in which you received the best grade. That was not an accident. Human beings always gravitate to things they do well. So our job as leaders is to identify what our people do well and then to put them into jobs that take advantage of that strength. I personally do not believe in the concept of putting someone in a job to build

an "opportunity for improvement." That hurts the individual, as they will be unhappy, and that hurts the organization, as we underutilize the person's talent.

Book reference:
Good to Great by Jim Collins

4. **Character is the most important trait of a leader.** At West Point I learned that the character of a leader is his or her most important attribute. Character is defined as always putting the needs of the organization above your own. As a captain in the army, I always ate after the soldiers in my command. At P&G, the leader should always take personal responsibility for results of his or her organization. As a West Point plebe (freshman) I learned that I was only permitted four answers: yes, no, no excuse, and I do not understand. These four answers are about character; there is no opportunity for equivocation or excuse; there is no "but."

    At West Point I also learned to **"choose the harder right instead of the easier wrong."** This powerful line comes from the West Point cadet prayer. Have you ever noticed how it is easier to do wrong things than right things? A leader who lives by his or her word can be counted on to do the unpopular thing when it is right. To always follow "the harder right," a leader must truly believe that a life directed by moral guidelines promises deeper and richer satisfaction than a self-serving, self-absorbed life. Living up to this ideal of character requires courage, determination, integrity, and self-discipline. You must live by your word and actions and know that is the most powerful demonstration of leadership.

Book references:
The West Point Way of Leadership by Col. Larry Donnithorne
West Point Cadet Prayer Book

5. **Diverse groups of people are more innovative than homogenous groups.** Diversity is a necessity at P&G to reflect the consumers we serve and to drive innovation, one of our five core strengths. Innovation is the result of connections and collaboration. James Burke, science historian and author/producer of *Connections*, documented that innovation often comes from connecting

two seemingly disconnected ideas. A diverse group is better able to make these connections since they have a greater diversity of nodes to connect. The role of the leader is to create the environment for connections and collaboration to occur. Leaders of the most effective diverse teams follow the "Platinum Rule": treat others as they want to be treated. The leader should know the people he or she works with well enough to know how they want to be treated.

Book reference:
Connections by James Burke

6. **Ineffective systems and cultures are bigger barriers to achievement than the talent level of the employees.** In total-quality training we all learned how difficult it was to pick up the right proportion of red and blue beads if the device we were using to pick them up was rigged to get a bad result. Similarly, Peter Senge teaches in his best-selling book *The Fifth Discipline* that "structure influences behavior," and systems often result in unintended consequences. For example, rent controls in New York to help the poor who lived in substandard housing actually further reduced investment to upgrade the housing, hurting the people the rent controls were designed to help. The role of leaders is to improve the systems and the cultures in which their organizations operate to improve the consistency and level of success of the results. Any high-performance organization must have four components: passionate leadership, sound strategies, robust systems, and a high-performance culture. A leader needs to work on all four pillars.

Book reference:
The Fifth Discipline by Peter Senge
Out of the Crisis by Edwards Deming

7. **There will be some people in the organization who will not make it on the journey.** Even after taking all of the steps above, there will still be some people in the leader's organization who will be either unwilling or unable to go on the journey of growth with the leader and the organization. It could be the sales manager who thinks you took away his job by eliminating price/volume negotiation or by getting rid of temporary price reduction. Or it could

be the individual for whom it is impossible to find the right job. A clue to finding these individuals is to find who is not happy day to day. It is the leader's job to identify those who cannot go on the journey, help them recognize the tension, and help them identify other careers that offer greater promise.

8. **Organizations must renew themselves.** Any organization, as with any organism that is growing, must renew itself. Growth, by definition, requires change. Change requires renewal. The standards of performance acceptable today will be unacceptable tomorrow if the organization is growing and improving. As such, the leader must provide training and development opportunities for the individuals in the organization to grow. Renewal is particularly important in a "promote from within" company like P&G. We need a healthy level of attrition within P&G to provide future opportunities for growth for our more junior employees.

Book reference:
Leading Change by John Kotter
The 7 Habits of Highly Effective People by Stephen Covey

9. **Recruiting is top priority.** There is nothing more important than recruiting. When we recruit, we are hiring the future leaders of the company and also our future friends. It is the source of growth of the company as we continually hire more talented people over time. The leader needs to be active in recruiting to ensure we are constantly raising standards and to gauge the level of renewal of the organization.

10. **The true test of the leader is the performance of the organization when they are absent or after they depart.** The leader's job is to build sufficient organization capability, including the leadership and individual initiative of the members of the organization, as well as the strategies/systems/culture of the organization, so that the leader's presence or absence would not significantly affect the business results. This means that the organization will be able to sustain itself successfully over time regardless of the quality of the leader.

Book reference:
Built to Last by Jim Collins

CHAPTER 5

Developing an Award-Winning Résumé

Contributed by Sharon Williams, M.Ed., World's Best Résumé Writer
Sharon Williams is a world-renowned résumé expert, career consultant, college instructor, and entrepreneur from Findlay, Ohio.

The owner of JobRockit, Sharon is a Certified Professional Résumé Writer (CPRW) and a member of Career Directors International (CDI). She is a thirteen-time National Winner of *Best Résumé/Cover Letter Honors*, including Best Executive Résumé, Best New Graduate Résumé and Cover Letter, Best Law Enforcement/Security, and Most Creative.

Most recently, Sharon earned the "World's Best Résumé Writer" designation (Professional Vote) for the first-ever worldwide résumé-writing contest sponsored by CDI.

Needless to say, Sharon Williams knows a thing or two about developing a great résumé.

Developing an Award-Winning Résumé: The Process is Key!

By Sharon Pierce-Williams, MEd, CPRW, and World's Best Résumé Writer

Whether you are a college student or a C-level executive, your résumé must be a persuasive, powerful, and differentiated presentation of who you are and what you have to offer. Since your résumé has only seconds to make a first impression on prospective employers, it is important to immediately show the value that you bring to the table. The goal of a résumé is to command employers' attention long enough to kindle interest and to generate interviews. So how do you showcase years of experience, education, community involvement, and empirical knowledge to create a competitive edge in a tough job market?

Let's get started!

A résumé is only as good as the information gathered.

By now, you may have earned certifications and awards, been evaluated by professors, employers, or colleagues, gained knowledge from internships or life experiences, and/or achieved great things on the job, in the classroom, through community service, or in various affiliations. Place this information and documentation in your "I love me" folder...and keep it up to date (evaluations, e-mails that say "good job," reference letters, etc.). For obvious reasons, keep the folder at home, not at work.

When I work with clients, I do not ask for addresses, education, or places worked (this information can be gathered from old documentation or through e-mails and phone calls later), but for information that will take a great deal of thought. I want the "best of who they are" first! Here's the initial information needed to prepare a dynamic, rough-draft shell of a résumé...

The Discovery Process

1. Review your old résumé (if you have one).

2. Write down your greatest hits (what you believe to be main contributions or accomplishments to date in your job/career, classroom, community, etc., and relevant to your targeted position). Here are some examples:

    Effective Leader: Led 40+ deal teams coordinating all facets of the transaction while managing internal and external expectations for closing. Selected by senior leadership team to serve on the Business Advisory Council and Training Committee—currently leading the Peer Learning Initiative for analysts, associates and assistant vice presidents

    Ability to Execute: Led underwriting process and closed ~40 real-estate deals ($650MM total volume) since 2011; portfolio manager for ~30 deals ($500MM portfolio value)

    Scholarship Athlete: Letterman on University Football team, achieved all-conference academic honor roll every season and recognized on the Chancellor's List

3. Challenge-Action-Result scenarios (CARs). It takes considerable thought and precise wording to showcase your value and qualifications. CARs are proof of "who you are" and tell a story as to "how you accomplish your goals." CARs can be developed from one or more of your "top ten greatest hits," and, remember, CARs should contain strengths required for your specific job/career target.

    The "challenge" should be no more than a couple of sentences to give an overview of the situation. The first sentence often begins with the word "To."

    The "action" should be listed as bullet points that describe the actions you took individually or as a team player to meet those challenges.

    The "results" (business impact) should be quantifiable or, at least, observable (e.g., college internships where knowledge gained becomes a transferable skill). For example, quantifiable results indicate how you saved a company money, increased efficiency in a process, solved a specific problem, or attracted new customers.

4. Endorsements written by superiors, colleagues, customers, vendors, or any person who can attest to your work ethic, strengths, and achievements, are an essential component of your résumé. Adding an endorsement to your résumé is like a stamp of approval or an exclamation mark. While some will say these references should not be on résumés, I've had executives request them once they see how the testimonials give such validation to CARs.

    The following are examples of performance endorsements:

    As [name of organization] advisor, Andy's participation in [name of organization] shows a work ethic above and beyond the average student. His professionalism, intellectual ethic, and desire to excel in all endeavors will make him a great asset to future employers.

    —John Smith, Director of Economics and Finance, University of North Carolina

    Jill expects the best from those around her and, by example, gets it. We were given a seemingly impossible task, and Jill brought together

a team that met and exceeded expectations. She gives direction and support and then stands back and watches the team perform. She expects and respects disagreements and manages to turn these into team-building opportunities.
—Senior Buyer, Hewlett Packard

5.   Targeted position/career objective. No résumé can be written without this! Enough said.

Drafting Your Résumé

Once you've gathered information from the five-step discovery process, determine the right format and begin creating your résumé draft.

It is time to start analyzing what sections are needed to showcase the individual. Create a header that includes your name, campus/current address, permanent address, phone number, and e-mail address (one that is professional). Make sure your name is in a font and size that exudes confidence.

Sell yourself with a powerful, succinctly written profile to immediately display your skills and achievements. Summarize the skill set gleaned from your work experience, school projects, community involvement, organizational leadership, and internships. Key words specific to your industry are vital in this section—speak the employer's language!

Quantify your accomplishments. It takes considerable thought and precise wording to showcase your value and qualifications to prove that you are the perfect match for the prospective employer's needs. Rather than stating job descriptions under Work Chronology, Affiliations, or Leadership Accomplishments, list quantifiable data to verify that you do make a difference. Hiring managers do not care about your past job responsibilities; they do care about what you achieved.

Easy-to-read format. This will allow the reader to quickly identify your skills and accomplishments.

The strategies listed above can be implemented to give you the edge needed to secure interviews. Also, keep in mind that the "P" words—persistence, polish, proof, persuasiveness, powerful profiles, presentation, and, most of all, passion—will lead to placement in a job that you've earned.

CHAPTER 6

Networking—More Than the Latest Buzzword

By Garrett D'Ottavio, Brand Manager, Unilever

It's Not Who You Know. It's Who Knows You

You were born into the world, and suddenly, without any effort at all, you joined your first network—family. These people would do anything for you as you grew—cook your food, clean your grass-stained clothes, or help with difficult homework assignments. When you had a question about anything, you would ask and trust the answers they gave you. The ability to ask any question and trust any answer is the basis of an ideal connection. Think "comfort" and "trust."

Now that you are aware of the dynamics that create a successful network, realize that the growth of this group of family, friends, and advisors will only grow if you take proactive steps for expansion. Taking the initiative to increase the number of people you can rely on is rooted in one idea—going above and beyond what others expect. (Sound familiar? You are reading this book, aren't you?)

In the case of relationships, at this point in your life, you are aware that quality is to be preferred over quantity. Being familiar with a large number of people but sincerely trusting few of them is not preferable when you could instead have a smaller group of individuals you keep in touch with and can rely on for anything. This is not to say that acquaintances are not worth your time; they are wonderful to have on your side. Still, those you trust for advice and assistance to shape your life—socially, romantically, scholastically, and professionally—this is the group you want to trust absolutely.

Understanding the inner workings of a network, you might take a step back and question why someone would or would not fit in your group of life advisors. Perhaps you even wonder how to add someone to this group. The fact is, having something in common is what brings people together, whether it is starting a conversation or evolving a friendship.

Building a More Reliable Network Than AT&T

After taking the time to carefully build my own network, I think I've established several steps that make creating a network easier.

Here are four easy steps to networking:

1. Introduction and purpose

    After identifying some people you know who have common interests, start a conversation with them; let them know what you hope to do and how you believe they could help you. There is no need to be incredibly blunt, but someone will realize quickly if you are trying to use him or her shamelessly. The purpose of having a network and being able to leverage it is that all parties involved should benefit at one point or another.

    For example, you realize Dr. Johnston, one of your professors, also works as a consultant at EyeBM, a company positioned in an industry you are interested in working in. You decide to ask him to review your résumé. After he reads your résumé, he gives you some great feedback on how to make your résumé more applicable to the industry. At the same time, one of Dr. J's coworkers at EyeBM recently made him aware of an internship opportunity. If you're a good student showing genuine interest in this company, don't you think Dr. Johnston will most likely pass your résumé along?

2. Ask

    Often the hardest part of networking is asking for help. Sure, it's easy to strike up a conversation with someone who has similar interests, but actually asking for help can be intimidating. There are a couple of things about human nature that may appease your concerns about asking someone to go out of his or her way for you:

- People like to help other people who are actually interested in doing something and who are taking an active approach to better their situation.
- When you go out of your way, you want to be appreciated, thanked, and kept in the loop about the long-term effects of your assistance.

Make your intentions known.

After initiating a relationship with Mrs. Murphy, a knowledgeable contact working in an industry (e.g., consumer packaged goods) in which you would like to work, you decide to ask her if she had a contact in HR at Murphy Co. (the company she works for). You go on to explain that you hoped she could help you get your résumé in front of an HR recruiter in order to review your résumé. It is important to let someone know your goals (e.g., getting your résumé in front of a Murphy Co. recruiter). Let them know you've done your research, you think you would mesh well with the company culture and values, and you want to apply for the job.

3. Appreciation and thanks

By now, you have established a relationship and asked a favor of another person you trust. Perhaps the most important steps remain. At this point, you have exactly what you wanted. Still, think about the other person in this equation; he or she went out of his or her way to help you. Remember, appreciation and thanks are two very different things. You can appreciate what this person has done for you, but in order to convey your gratitude, you need to thank them, and in a timely fashion.

How do you make yourself stand out? (Success is all about standing out and making people remember you—in a good way.)

Two words: handwritten thanks.

Regardless of the outcome, the individual who helped you needs to know how much you appreciate what they did. Write them a handwritten note (yes, pen, paper, envelope, and postage—the old-fashioned way), and send it by mail. Ask yourself what is more meaningful and memorable—a brief e-mail that took five to ten seconds to write and send, or a handwritten note that someone took the time to write to sincerely thank you? Small gestures like this go a long way in business.

4. Keep in touch and give back

Make sure to keep in touch with these people. Alluding to a point I made not long ago, when people help you, they are probably interested in hearing about the effects of what they did for you. Let them know where you are as a result of their help, and don't be shy to thank them again for helping.

Could this step be awkward? Seemingly, yes. Create a genuine relationship, and it won't be. Send a shameless request on a yearly basis, and it will be. Take this route instead: every month or two, send a link to an article you read online that covers a common interest, take the opportunity to ask them how they are doing, and share a sentence or so about what you're currently working on. This type of update comes off as caring, curious, and genuine.

Lastly, let's not forget that people like to help, but networks and favors are a two-way street. Make sure this person understands not only that you appreciate their help but also that you are willing to assist them in any way you can. Just commenting that you are willing to help is different from what I am suggesting. Anyone can tell them that, but you're not trying to be anyone. You are trying to separate yourself from the pack. Be specific. Think of a way you could benefit this person. Who could you connect them to from your network? What book did you read that you think they may benefit from? The list goes on. Be creative.

You begin an internship with Proctor & Gamble (one that you interviewed for as a result of your contact, Charles, putting your résumé on a desk in HR). Then you find out about a great new blog that addresses subject matter relevant to your company. After a month or so of no contact, you send an e-mail to Charles, thanking him again and offering a brief summary of what you're doing. Additionally, you offer the site address to this blog because you think it would be interesting to him. Ask Charles what he is up to and whether he would be available for lunch, and make sure to make it obvious you are always willing to help him out if he needs something.

If I Were a Potential Connection, Where Would I Be?

There are a number of venues to build a network, tangible and virtual.

Initially, wrap your mind around the idea that the sort of people you want in your network are the go-getters. Connecting with someone who hates his or her job and does just enough to get by is not who you want to associate with for advice and recommendations.

Now you know who you are after—high achievers in an industry you are interested in. You can find these people, physically, by going to events like trade shows, conferences, or even by contacting an HR representative of a company requesting a shadowing opportunity. The more you get out of your comfort zone, the more you will stand out from your peers.

In a virtual sense, networking sites like LinkedIn are a wonderful resource. I won't bore you with the ins and outs of the site because creating a profile and making connections is fairly self-explanatory—but I will share a great strategy with you: leverage alumni.

It's safe to say that when you graduate, you'll have at least some school spirit. Maybe you won't be at every home football game, but picture yourself sitting at your desk, doing the same kind of work you always do, when someone from your university contacts you with a plea for advice on getting into your industry. Naturally you are a bit excited. Now you get to catch up on what's happening on campus: new buildings, how's the hockey team doing, etc. The fact is, alumni want to help out. After all, they were in your position not too long ago. Leverage this connection on LinkedIn, but also in general. Contact your alumni office, and ask for a list of professionals in the industry you want to be and actually call them! Most of them list information for precisely this reason. They want to help!

Here is a LinkedIn tip: After creating a profile you are proud of (take some time to do this, because the profile represents you and can be found on a search engine), play around with the search function.

1. In quotations, type in your school's name.
2. Add a company you are interested in working for.
3. If you have a location in mind, add that too.
4. Now you should have a pretty specific group of people. They went to your university, work somewhere, or work in an industry you have an interest in, and possibly, in a city you like.
5. Do some Facebook-style stalking (we've all had our practice). Figure out which of these people you genuinely want to interact with and request to connect with them.
6. In your "Invitation to Connect" (which is basically an e-mail-like personal message sent to the contact), make sure to tell this person the following, briefly:

- Who you are
- That you attend or attended their alma mater
- That you are interested in hearing about their professional journey since college
- That you would appreciate any advice they might have for you

Here's a final tip: You only have a limited number of words, so write concisely and with a purpose.

As a result of this request, you should have a decent percentage of individuals who get back to you—some of whom could be great resources and connections as you try to find internships and jobs.

At this point I think you understand the basic steps of networking. I have just a few more tips to offer you:

- Remember to not be shy when it comes to asking for help. You have to ask if you want to receive (but there's a way to go about it, as you now know, that can benefit both parties).
- The best time to network is when you don't need anything. Make some contacts in your industry on the basis of curiosity of best practices or advice. Maybe one day when you need someone, you'll already have a genuine friend to ask.
- People like to be around those who are polite and appreciative. Sure, you can get ahead by using someone and pretending to care about helping them. But instead of burning that bridge, how about working on enhancing it, so you can both leverage it down the road.

Uncommon Common Sense

After digesting those last few pages, you may say, "Big deal. This is common sense." True, it is common sense...but how "common" is it really? How many people are genuine in their intentions to benefit both parties, to send a handwritten thank you, and to actually stay in touch? I will absolutely concede these suggestions as common sense, but act on these ideas, and suddenly you're not so common—wasn't that the point all along?

CHAPTER 7
Career Fair Essentials

Early and Often

When it comes to career fairs and job preparation, it's essential to start early and practice often. Falling into the commonly held mentality that freshman and sophomores don't need to attend career fairs is your first mistake. There's a laundry list of excuses:

- I'm too young; there aren't any opportunities for freshman and sophomores.
- Career fairs are for seniors; I don't need to worry about that yet.
- I have a class at the same time—I can't afford to miss it.
- I don't have a suit.
- I haven't had a chance to create a résumé.

Save it. The excuses not to go are endless in number. But, the truth is, you can't afford *not* to attend. In this chapter, we'll provide a high-level career fair timeline and explore how you should prepare yourself for interfacing with potential employers.

The Four-Year Game Plan

For the average freshman, attending the university's career fair is generally pretty far down on the priority list. If your goal is to be extraordinary, this is great news. This is another opportunity to set yourself apart.

In this chapter, we'll discuss the benefits of attending a career fair and how to use the "Four-Year Game Plan" as your guide to career fair success.

Freshman Year: The Year of Discovery

Most college freshmen have never been to or even heard of a career fair. There's nothing wrong with that. Don't let the lack of experience be a source of anxiety or intimidation. (If you're a senior and you still haven't been, feel free to be nervous. Just kidding. But not really.) As a freshman, simply showing up will help alleviate this fear. Remember that 90 percent of life is showing up.

Your freshman year should be a time of exploration and discovery. There is *no pressure* when you're a freshman. Take advantage of it. The companies you speak with will be extremely impressed that a freshman took the initiative and showed up.

While attending the career fair as a freshman, you should do the following:

- Take note of the setup and organization.
- Talk with several companies. Learn more about the opportunities they offer. Chances are they won't offer internships to freshman, but they will be impressed you are attending simply to learn about different internship/career opportunities. This level of maturity will help you in subsequent years.
- Practice, practice, practice. Present to companies with nothing on the line. It's much easier to practice as a freshman than a senior who needs to get a job.
- Ask for feedback. Let recruiters know you are a freshman, and then ask them for input on how you did and what they are looking for in an employee. They will gladly give it to you.

Participating as a freshman puts you ahead of the curve. This type of initiative sets you up for success later in life.

Sophomore Year: The Year of Improvement

If you took the initiative as a freshman to attend the career fair and got the lay of the land, you've put yourself in a great position for year two. Sophomore year is a little different; this year should be used to improve your communication skills and convey professionalism.

It used to be that employers targeted only rising seniors for internship positions, but recently more and more companies are offering these opportunities to rising juniors (current sophomores). With a majority of internships serving as pipelines for full-time employment opportunities, sophomores should pursue *question-mark internships*.

Explore a question-mark field. For example, as a finance major, you may have an interest in investment banking, but you aren't sure the money is worth the long, grueling hours. An internship with an investment banking (IB) firm will give you the opportunity to experience life in IB for three months.

It's important to remember that an internship is a two-way tryout. For a finite amount of time, a company gets to try you out as an employee, and you get to evaluate them and the career opportunities they present.

Junior Year: The Year of Positioning

This is where the rubber meets the road. Junior year is the time to select the internship that hopefully feeds into a full-time offer. Once again, internships should be approached as pipelines for full-time positions; many quality interns are offered a job at the conclusion of their duty. As a junior attending a career fair, research and rank your top three or top five companies. Then, seek out their internships as you would a full-time job. Be confident, and present yourself as the best possible candidate. Don't give them a reason to turn you down!

Senior Year: The Year of Relaxation

You're probably thinking, "Shouldn't this be the most important year?" As a freshman, you observed and learned; as a sophomore, you tried something new and different; and as a junior, you successfully completed an internship and perhaps received a full-time offer. As a senior, hopefully you have a job lined up, giving you no reason to attend a career fair—let the year of relaxation begin!

We know that this is the ideal situation, and not all students are fortunate enough to begin their senior year with a job. If you didn't receive an offer or decided you wanted to pursue another opportunity, approach senior year at the career fair with the same level of preparation and confidence you showed as a junior. By now, you are a career fair veteran and know exactly what you need to do to achieve success.

Career Fair 101: An All-Inclusive Guide

Precareer fair, do your homework.

- Get a list of the companies attending. This is typically located on the school's website or in the career services office.
- Identify the companies/internships/programs in which you are interested and then research the following:
  - Internship description
  - Length of program
  - Career opportunities
  - Company values
  - Candidate requirements (e.g., minimum GPA, leadership skills, etc.)
  - Qualities they are looking for in a great candidate
- Create your own personal "information packet" (See below).
- Plot your course. Get a map showing the locations of company tables.
- Determine your order. If you plan on talking to six or seven companies, be sure to stop by one or two "warm-ups." These are companies that you don't have much interest in, but talking to their recruiters will help you relax and practice before approaching your targeted opportunities.

Below is a sample of a company profile in your Career Fair Information Packet. We'll use General Electric as our example.

- Company: General Electric
- Targeted program: Financial management program
  - Program Summary
    - Intensive two-year entry-level program spanning four rotational assignments

- Hands-on experience may include financial planning, accounting, operations analysis, auditing, forecasting, treasury/cash management, commercial finance, and business development.
- Combines coursework, job assignments, and interactive seminars to equip you with exceptional technical, financial, and business skills
- Courses led by senior GE professionals and mentors
- Develops world-class financial leaders for exciting positions
  - Preferred Criteria
    - Minimum 3.0 GPA/mobility
    - Leadership experience
    - Communication skills
    - Finance major/past internships
  - Key Contacts
    - Bob Smith (Bob.Smith@ge.com)
    - Jane Johnson (Jane.Johnson@ge.com)
  - Questions
    - What is a typical summer project for an FMP intern?
    - What locations/GE businesses are hiring FMP interns for next summer?
    - What do you like most about working for GE?
  - Comments/Notes

You're only helping yourself by putting together a simple page for every company you plan on approaching at the career fair. Creating these one-page summaries forces you to do the following:

- Research the company's internship and career opportunities and determine if they match your professional goals.
- Determine the company's preferred criteria. This helps you develop a pitch tailored to what the company values in a candidate.
- Develop Questions. This is extremely important for continuing the conversation with the recruiter after your initial introduction and avoiding the infamous awkward silence.

- Provide space for comments and notes. Make sure you write down key take-aways from the conversation including the recruiter's name, internship opportunities, follow-up procedures, etc.

The thirty-second pitch: delivering an effective introduction

Researching the companies and programs of interest is very important, but it's only the first step. Effectively articulating a thirty-second introduction that will set you apart from the other hundreds of students the recruiter will speak to throughout the day is paramount. How are you going to do this? You guessed it—research and preparation.

Research

If you've done your homework, you're in good shape. Some areas to make sure you cover are as follows:

- Internship program and company specifics
- What they're looking for in an ideal candidate (qualities, skills, background, and experience)
- Further questions you want answered

Preparation

Use your research to prepare for your thirty-second pitch. Believe it or not, most students attend career fairs without so much as looking at a company website, fully expecting to learn everything from the recruiters. While one of the recruiter's jobs is to educate you about their company, it's far more impressive for a student to approach a recruiter's table with some foundational knowledge. Here is a rough outline of how to structure your pitch:

- Introduce yourself (name/major).
- Articulate the specific internship or full-time position that interests you.
- Have a few questions ready to keep the conversation going. The recruiter will engage you with some questions; however, it's more impressive if you are able to ask intelligent questions, as it makes the recruiter's job that much easier.

Sample Pitch

Start off with a simple, casual greeting: "Hi, my name is Jon Buehner. I'm junior finance major." Hand the recruiter your résumé, and say, "I've done some reading about your leadership training programs, and I'm interested learning more about the FMP program, the one targeted specifically for finance majors. Could you tell me a little more about the internship?"

Observe how the pitch was structured: introduction, interest, open-ended question. By asking this type of question, you have done two things: shifted the conversation back to the recruiter and made the recruiter's job easier by posing a question (so he or she doesn't have to come up with one). After hearing the recruiter's response, have several follow-up questions ready. Remember, the goal is to be memorable in a good way. Examples of intelligent follow-up questions include:

- In completing the FMP Internship, would I have an opportunity to interview for a full-time position? Does the internship feed into a full-time program?
- What are the next steps in order to be eligible to apply for the internship?

In some cases, it's okay if you already know the answers. By doing your research and developing insightful questions tailored to their programs, you are already gaining points with the recruiter.

Appropriate dress: less is more
   Business professional attire—Be conservative!
- Men should wear a suit (black, gray, or navy), a conservative tie, and polished shoes.
- Women should wear a suit (black, gray, or navy), a conservative shirt, and low-to-medium heels.

What to bring: the essentials
   Here's a short list of what you should bring to the career fair:
- Leather-bound portfolio, which can be purchased in your campus bookstore for twenty to twenty-five dollars
- Copies of your résumé (at least two copies for every company you plan on speaking with), printed on thirty-two-pound résumé paper
- A pen or pencil

- Business cards (if you have them)
- Your "career fair research packet"

Put your résumés in the left-side pocket of the portfolio and your "CFR Packet" on the right side for easy note taking. (All you southpaws out there should do the opposite.) Just remember to only bring the essentials. It's difficult and awkward to interact with recruiters when your hands are full of stuff you don't need. Resist the urge to carry around all the free pens, stuffed animals, Post-it note holders, highlighters, wipe and write boards, stress reliever balls, luggage tags, t-shirts, stickers, folders, and other promotional materials that recruiters will try to hand out to you. Kindly accept it, and then toss them away before you go to the next recruiter.

1. Arrival time: It all depends.
   Don't stress too much about when to arrive. As I mentioned in the subtitle of the section, it all depends on your circumstances. Consider the following:
   - Are you planning to speak with several companies? If so, allot the necessary amount of time.
   - Do you have a class that you can't miss? Arrive after class if it's early in the day. Wear your suit, and go straight from class…don't waste any time.
   - Busy in the middle. Keep in mind that the career fair will peak and be the most crowded about halfway through. If you plan on talking to a popular employer, plan on getting there early.

2. While you're there
   The day is finally here. Most students are scrambling to dig out their suits, printing their résumés (or creating one), determining whom they want to meet, and figuring out the day's schedule. Fortunately, you're prepared and focused on what's important. You have completed the research, mapped out your course, and prepared and practiced your pitch. The hard part is over. Go close the deal.

Talking to Employers: Prep, Pitch, Prolong

Keep it simple. Limit the variability. Make it easy on yourself by following a formula: thirty seconds of prep, thirty-second pitch, prolong.

Thirty-Second Prep

Take thirty seconds to look over your notes to refresh your memory. Note the employer basics, the opportunity/internship/full-time program, and the questions you have prepared.

Thirty-Second Pitch

Approach the employer's table, engage and greet the employer (firm handshake and eye contact), and deliver your thirty-second pitch. As indicated earlier, you should do the following:

- Introduce yourself (name/major).
- Briefly tell them what you are interested in (specific internship program/full-time position).

Prolong the Conversation

Have a couple of questions ready to keep the conversation going. The recruiter will engage you with some questions, but it's more impressive if you are able to ask intelligent questions. Remember, your goal is to be remembered (in a good way, of course). When you are done talking, tell the employer "thanks" and ask for a business card. After walking away from the table, make some notes on the conversation.

The Other Side of the Table: A Recruiter's Perspective

By understanding how most companies recruit, you can better position yourself to get an interview. This isn't rocket science; the career fair recruitment methodology is relatively simple:

1. Recruiters talk with students and take their résumé.
2. After they finish talking with a student, the recruiter makes notes about the conversation on the back of the résumé and typically places it in one of two stacks: *Good* and *Bad*.
3. After the career fair is over (typically later that night), the recruiters sit together to go through the *Good* pile to determine who will be awarded an interview.

Don't put undue pressure on yourself, but think of your conversation with a recruiter as an informal interview. Regardless of the circumstance, you are *always* making an impression.

After You Get Home: A Few, Final Steps

When you get home, resist the urge to turn on the TV and crack open a beer for just for a few minutes (that Keystone Light isn't going anywhere). There are a few more steps you can take that can make a huge impact.

Thank You Notes

Write thank-you notes (e-mails work) to all the recruiters you spoke with. Their e-mail addresses should be on the business cards you collected. It's extremely important to send the e-mails as soon as you get home. Recruiters will most likely be making their decisions on who gets an interview that same night.

Set Your Agenda

Identify any necessary steps that you need to complete to move forward. For example, many companies require an online application, even though you may be participating in their campus recruitment. These seem like small steps, but the devil is always in the details!

CHAPTER 8

Interviewing to Land the Job

Interviewing the Interviewer: A Conversation with Robert Morrison

A Quick Bio: Robert Morrison, Former CEO, 3M, Quaker Oats, Kraft

Over the course of his career, Robert Morrison has interviewed thousands of candidates: undergraduates, MBAs, and seasoned executives. Mr. Morrison has served as chief executive officer and chairman for some of America's most respected corporations, including the Quaker Oats Company, Kraft Foods, and 3M. In addition to being a former captain in the US Marine Corps, Mr. Morrison is the chairman of the Museum of Science and Industry and a director and trustee for several civic, cultural, and business organizations in Chicago. He is also a member of the dean's council at the Kellogg Graduate School of Management at Northwestern University and holds a bachelor's degree in English from Holy Cross College and an MBA from Wharton Graduate School of Business at the University of Pennsylvania.

Full Preparation Is Essential

During our discussion, Mr. Morrison emphasized the importance of full preparation for success in an interview. He went on to explain that the preparation must be two-fold: as a candidate, a student must do the following:

1. Prepare to Know the Company
   The first part of "full preparation" is researching and truly knowing the company with which you are interviewing. This goes beyond knowing that Frito

Lay makes chips or Procter & Gamble makes soap. Student candidates should read through the following information prior to their interview:

- Company website. Click on every link to learn about the company's history, culture, lines of business, career opportunities, locations, management team, etc.
- Company annual report. This can typically be found on the company website and downloaded as a PDF file.
- Company 10-K and 10-Q. These are financial documents required by the SEC and can also be downloaded from the company website as PDF files.

You may not have time to read all these company reports cover to cover. Here are a few items to highlight from the reports, according to Mr. Morrison:

- Company management
  - Who is running the company?
  - What are the backgrounds of their employees?
  - How will this affect company culture?
- Ability to develop you
  - Will the company provide the structure you need for professional growth?
  - Will you be a more marketable professional after working at the company?
- Typical career path
  - What does a typical career look like with company X?
  - What opportunities are there for advancement?
  - Will your professional growth be limited?
  - Is the company a "career company," or do people come and work there for two or three years and leave?
  - What are typical salary levels at company X? Are they competitive with other companies in the industry?

These are the questions you must ask and the answers you must seek in order to fully understand the company that is interviewing you. As you read through the questions, you may realize that all the answers may not be easily found in company reports. Mr. Morrison emphasized the importance of reaching out to current employees to discover what the company is all about. It is only by putting forth a little extra effort and doing the necessary research that students can truly understand the company and fully prepare for the interview.

2. Prepare to Know Yourself

    Your first reaction is probably, "I already know myself; why do I have to prepare?" While this might seem like common sense, Mr. Morrison explained that most undergraduates have not mastered the ability to effectively convey their accomplishments in a concise and professional manner. It's one thing to know "you were president of your fraternity," but that's not enough. You must be capable of conveying your accomplishments. Can you quantify how you improved the fraternity during your tenure? What new programs did you create to benefit the membership? These are the types of questions you should be able to answer in order to truly "know yourself."

    Mr. Morrison talked about knowing yourself by showing the difference between how "Undergraduate Jon" and "MBA Jon" would respond to a posed interview question.

    Scenario 1: Undergraduate Jon

    > Interviewer: Jon, can you tell me a little bit about your involvement on campus?
    >
    > [This is a relatively simple question, requiring a student candidate to know him or herself.]
    >
    > Undergraduate Jon: Well...I was the president of my business fraternity...and...uh...was a member of this finance club where we had speakers each week.

    Scenario 2: MBA Jon

    > Interviewer: Jon, can you tell me a little bit about your involvement on campus?
    >
    > MBA Jon: Bob, I am really glad you asked that question. As a member of Pi Sigma Epsilon, a professional business fraternity, I had the opportunity to gain great leadership experience holding three leadership positions: director of corporate relations, vice president of communications, and most recently, president. As president, I built a strong foundation for our membership by creating and implementing eight new professional development events, including: résumé workshops, a precareer-fair night, career coaching and an executive-speaker series.

    This scenario was stretched to the extreme to make a point because this is something Mr. Morrison has seen time and time again. Undergraduate candidates often have great résumés but simply do not know how to effectively sell themselves to the interviewer. Mr. Morrison says, "Students must learn to relate their past achievements and experience to the tasks they would be assigned as future employees of that company. Through dedicated self-examination, students can improve their ability to talk about their accomplishments and interview like an MBA."

3.   Don't Order a Coke at Your Interview with Pepsi
     At one point during our discussion, Mr. Morrison laughed, saying, "And don't forget...Don't order a Coke when you are interviewing with Pepsi." This might seem like common sense, but it's the type of silly mistake that will guarantee you don't get the job. Here is a quick story he told us about a young man who was interviewing for a job with a prestigious advertising firm:

> When the interviewer asked the candidate, "So, what are some ads that you like?" Confidently, the young man quickly answered identifying two television ad campaigns. He proceeded to give a thorough analysis of why he liked the ads and why he felt they accurately appealed to the correct target market. The young man did an exceptional job answering the question and was able to provide accurate reasoning on why he thought the ad was well done. Unfortunately, the two ads the young man chose were created by a rival ad agency...You can imagine how the rest of the interview went. Despite his impressive résumé, the young man did not get the job. Learn to know your audience.

4.   Forget What Your Mom Taught You—for Just Fifteen Minutes
     If you grew up with parents like mine, you were taught "not to brag" and to "be humble." These are great life lessons to learn and practice; however, Mr. Morrison heavily stressed the importance of self-promotion:

> Forget what your mom taught you for at least fifteen minutes. I am positive you have a number of impressive accomplishments; otherwise the company wouldn't want to interview you. The interview is your time to promote yourself...and yes, brag a little. Make sure you are assertive, be confident, sit up straight, make good eye contact, and remember that interviewers are looking for accomplished people.

5. What to Expect: Five Questions Asked Fifty Different Ways

One of the most beneficial interview preparation techniques is anticipating the questions and developing examples to use for each response. This is not as difficult as it may seem. When you boil it down, there are about five interview questions asked fifty different ways. Mr. Morrison highlighted five topics that repeatedly pop up in interview questions:

- Greatest strength/accomplishments?
- Greatest weakness/failure?
- What draws you to our company?
- Problem solving—how did you help solve the problem?
- Setting yourself apart—how are you different than all the other candidates?

If you are able to anticipate these questions and develop succinct responses, tying in your personal accomplishments to help answer the question, you will stack up favorably against the competition.

The importance of preparation cannot be understated, but at times interviewers will ask prospects a few off-the-wall questions to see how they respond. During our meeting, Mr. Morrison shared a time when he was asked, "If you could sit down and spend time with three people from the twentieth century, who would they be and why?" These questions can either derail students during an interview or give them a chance to show their creativity. Make sure you are on your toes! A few common questions include the following:

- What was the last book you read?
- What do you like to do in your free time?
- What can you tell me about the Affordable Care Act (or any highly relevant current event)?

6. Interviewing the Interviewer

At the end of most interviews, the interviewer will ask the candidates if they have any questions. Answering "no" is the worst possible response. Have a few questions in mind before the interview. If you think of an intelligent question during your interview, don't be afraid to ask it. Do not ask fact-based questions you could find on the company website. Mr. Morrison provided

INTERVIEWING TO LAND THE JOB

the following advice for candidates to help them develop meaningful postinterview questions:

- Don't ask one-word questions—try to ask open-ended, general questions.
- Make sure questions show you are intent on being exceptional at the company.
  1. What qualities set people apart in this company/program?
  2. What keeps people at company X? What do people like about working at your company?
  3. What is a typical career progression in the _____ field?

You will most likely have the opportunity to ask only one or two questions. Therefore, it is not too important to develop ten postinterview questions.

7. A Quick Review
   - Know the company; know yourself.
   - Sell yourself and your accomplishments.
   - Anticipate the questions, and prepare your responses.

These simple steps will set you apart from the rest of school and help you interview like an MBA!

80

CHAPTER 9
The Power of Internships

A Two-Way Tryout

nternship is a word you've probably heard for years. But what is it, really? Simply put, an internship is a temporary position that provides students the opportunity to gain valuable work experience in a specific field. Most of the time, internships are completed during a ten- to twelve-week stretch during the summer, but some can last for a semester or even a year, depending on the program.

Internships aren't just for business students either. They're offered in a variety of different career fields such as medicine, architecture, nonprofits, and government organizations, among many others. And they can be paid or unpaid, depending on the program.

Instead of thinking about your responsibilities as "the intern," think of this opportunity as a two-way tryout. Always remember, you are trying out the company and they are trying out you.

Over the course of the internship, decide if you enjoy the type of work you are doing. Is the company culture conducive to your personality? Could you see yourself working here full-time? At the end of your internship, the company may offer you a full-time position upon graduation. If you are serious about getting a sought-after job, completing an internship is a great first step.

The Four-Year Game Plan

As you begin your homework on internship opportunities, consider creating a four-year game plan to help get your thoughts, interests, and goals on paper.

Freshman to Sophomore Year

Already? Yes. Larger companies and corporations typically look for older students with more experience for their internship positions, but great opportunities exist with small or midsized companies. At this point in the process, try to leverage any contacts you already have. For example, your friend's mom works in human resources for company X near your hometown, and she can get you an interview for an internship. Take advantage of this opportunity! This is an investment in your career. It shows initiative and provides experience most other candidates won't have when interviewing for a highly competitive internship at a larger company.

Sophomore to Junior Year

This is your opportunity to try something different.

Who do you think is more appealing to an employer? A finance major who did three internships in finance and who only knows finance, or a well-rounded finance major who spent one summer as a marketing intern and another in an ancillary field? Furthermore, do you know exactly what you want to do with your life at twenty years of age? Think of this year as your chance to become a well-rounded individual.

Junior to Senior Year

By now, you've had a few years to think about what you want to do when you graduate. As a rising senior, this is the time to land an internship at a company, or at least in a field, where you could see yourself working full time after college. Remember, summer internships are often pipelines for full-time candidates. It's not unheard of for the summer internship to land you a full-time job before you return to campus for your senior year.

Internships: The Building Blocks of Your Future Career
Start Your Search Early

Give yourself the best chance of landing a great internship by preparing early. This can be as simple as doing the following:

1. Constructing your résumé
2. Writing a cover Letter

3.   Attending a university career fair
4.   Actively networking
5.   Job-shadow a professional in a career-field that interests you

Take Advantage of Opportunities

During the internship, take full advantage of the great opportunities you will have.

1.   Learn as much as you can from your mentor.
2.   Take on as much responsibility as you are allowed.
3.   Seek out additional professional development opportunities.
4.   Job-shadow a colleague for a day.
5.   Build relationships with the current employees.
6.   Attend any workshops or seminars offered.
7.   Be proactive!

Use a variety of outlets to search for internship opportunities. Company websites, career services at your college or university, family, and friends can all be great resources. We wish you the best of luck as you begin your search!

CHAPTER 10

Backpacks to Briefcases

M ark Liston is the Vice President of Success Group International Sales and Marketing at Valpak.

Success Group International (SGI) helps independent contractors and business owners in the home services industry achieve greater success in their fields. Acting as a business school and consultant for their members, SGI has helped countless family-run businesses maximize their potential.

In his previous role, Mark was the Director of Sales Recruiting for Valpak, a North American direct marketing company that provides businesses with print and online advertising solutions and consumer coupons. Valpak has been a major sponsor of sales-focused college organizations around the country.

Backpacks to Briefcases

By Mark Liston

Twenty-five years from now, you will look back on this adventure and remember the transition you made to your first full-time gig out of college—when you went from the backpack world to the briefcase world. I would like to share six secrets with you that will help you with this transition.

Secret #1: Clean Up Your Online Image

The world of social networking has changed with the advent of sites such as Twitter, Facebook, and LinkedIn. By the time you are reading this, there will be, undoubtedly, many similar sites.

Not long ago we had a sixties murder mystery party at our home. My wife and I looked in the garage and in the closets and found several albums—those we had purchased in the 1960s and 1970s, when we were teenagers.

We also found our high school yearbooks—the class of '72. As I went through my yearbook, I found many irreverent things that my friends had written. Some were still very funny, but I certainly wouldn't have let my mom see them back then—or even today! There would have been no way that I would have ever allowed a potential employer to see them.

That brings us to Twitter and Facebook.

I don't think the humor today is much different than the early 1970s. The difference is that what used to be viewable to only those friends you chose can now be viewed by anyone with Internet access—even employers.

Back then there were Polaroid cameras when we wanted to see instant pictures—not digital cameras. And we couldn't download anything. It just wasn't cool to carry around a Polaroid camera at a party.

With social networking today, friends can post pictures of what happened last night because they took a picture of you with their cell phone. Yes, things are very different today than they were when I was making my transition from backpacks to briefcases.

Here is what's happening in the briefcase world. Potential employers are going to social networking sites and learning about you. They are doing this not to find ways of hiring you, but to see if there are reasons they *shouldn't* be hiring you!

In economic downturns, the workforce is overloaded with an abundance of experienced people who are applying for the same jobs you are. What you don't need is a potential employer going to a social networking site and seeing you dancing on the bar.

Is this to say that the people who are doing the research didn't do the same thing when they were your age? No! But that doesn't matter. Again, companies are looking for a reason to not hire versus reasons to hire.

So let's make this simple and provide you with an easy rule: "Don't upload anything to social networking sites that you wouldn't want your grandmother to see!" It's that easy!

This isn't to say you can't have a "private" place in social networking sites that you only allow your most trusted friends to visit. I repeat, *most trusted*. Just make sure you monitor the sites an employer can visit, and make sure it reveals what you would want a potential employer to see.

One more thing. If you are still in school and are using a "dot edu" e-mail address, get a Gmail or Yahoo! (or other) free e-mail address to use on your résumé. I have tried to reach hundreds of people I met after they graduated only to find that they were using a dot edu address, and my e-mails came bouncing back.

It is hard to hire someone to the briefcase world when they are using a backpack e-mail address that expired when they left school.

Secret #2: Take Advantage of Internships

According to *USA Today*, 84 percent of all students say they will do an internship. Employers reported nearly 36 percent of their new employees came from their own internship programs.

So what is the value of an internship program?

First, don't do it for the college credits. This isn't about getting credits to graduate; this is about getting the experience to go from backpacks to briefcases.

I look at an internship as simply getting an opportunity to see if you really like this profession or job. It's easy to become blinded by your excitement about an industry. Every job has its downsides. It's important to find out what those downsides are.

An internship should give you the opportunity to talk to people a couple years older than you who have opted for a briefcase at that company. They remember what it was like looking for a career. Those people can tell you what it's like working for that company on a full-time basis. They can talk to you about their secrets of success and a potential career path for you.

You also have a chance to make valuable contacts who could influence your career for the rest of your life. Remember, managers are always looking for talent that makes them look better. If you ask me who is the best person I have *ever* hired, and I've hired hundreds, I'll quickly tell you "Kevin." He makes me look brilliant!

You could work for someone who becomes a great mentor. This person may help you get a full-time position with the company after you graduate. This same person may change careers/companies at some point and want to bring you with her (all the more reason not to have a dot edu address).

Finally, internships give you an opportunity to see what the briefcase world is all about. You will interface with all kinds of people and learn what it takes to succeed in the briefcase world. *Office Space* is one of my favorite movies, but the briefcase world isn't really like that!

Here's the other side of the coin, which is looking at things from the employer's point of view. Providing an internship allows an employer to hire you at a low wage for what's essentially a ten- to twelve-week interview to determine if he or she wants to keep you on the team in the future. That's why so many new college grads are hired full-time after internship programs.

Secret #3: Always Be Coachable

Remember your ABCs.

You are from a generation that is comfortable having a coach. Many of you played on a sports team when you were five or six years old. Or you've had music lessons, dance lessons, or something similar.

Because of this you can turn a disadvantage into an advantage. Let me explain.

Recently I was talking with a recent grad who did an internship at a pharmaceutical company. She enjoyed the internship and couldn't wait to take a full-time position. After what seemed (to her) like an endless interview process, she was disappointed to hear that the company decided to hire someone who had a "couple years of experience."

Ahhhh—that nasty "we need someone with experience" line.

Here is the line that I wish everyone with little or no experience would use with me when I interview them (write this one down—internalize it.): "I am the most coachable person you will ever hire! I know I don't have any experience, but that is to your advantage, because you will be able to mold me into the employee that you want and need."

But here comes the hard part—you need to live it. You have to welcome the coaching. You need to remind your coach/mentor/boss that you relish constructive guidance because it just makes you better.

This brings us to a question. "If Tiger Woods believes he still needs a coach, don't you think that you, too, should be willing to have a coach?" If you were already the best in the world at your profession, would you be willing to change coaches to get even better? Tiger did!

Tiger Woods was the number one–ranked golfer in the world in 2002. Butch Harmon had been his coach for ten years. Then Tiger made a change and hired Hank Haney. Think about it. Tiger was already number one...on the planet! But he wanted to get better, and he was willing to make a change to get better.

There it is. There is the secret sauce. Still wondering what I'm saying? Okay, here it is. Remember your ABCs—"Always Be Coachable."

What does this have to do with a future employer? It's simple! Many of us who will hire and manage you are baby boomers. Do you know how many of us learned how to swim? Someone threw us in the lake! (This method helps you learn very fast!) How did we learn how to sell? We knocked on doors! How did we learn to ride a bike? Training wheels that eventually wore out.

So my generation was one that was awful at taking coaching! We didn't want it. We were perfectly happy to fail until we learned. Gen Xers were the cynical generation—the first latchkey kids, who saw their parents lose their jobs as companies closed and the word "downsizing" came into vogue. You can't tell Gen Xers what to do.

Here you are—this massive generation, almost eighty million strong—wanting to be coached! That is a breath of fresh air to us! We can't believe it. Someone will actually listen to us, do what we want, and become the employee that we need. No way!

Have you memorized this yet? "I am the most coachable person you will ever hire! I know I don't have experience, but that is to your advantage because you will be able to mold me into the employee that you want and need."

By the way, if those words don't work, use "Tiger Woods has a coach—why wouldn't I want one?" That might bring tears to your manager's eyes!

Secret #4: Don't Limit Your Base of Interest

Recently, my job involved hiring recent college grads who wanted a career in sales. It turned out that after I interviewed one hundred people and asked them, "What kind of sales job are you looking for?" the answer was invariably "pharmaceutical sales."

While doing some research about this type of sales, I tripped over the FierceBiotech website. One of their articles cited the top five layoffs of 2008 in the pharmaceutical industry. Over twenty thousand people were laid off—according to the article—at Merck, Shering-Plough, Wyeth, UCB Pharma, and AstraZeneca.

One of my fears is that today's graduating seniors are so focused on a single industry or a specific company that they don't listen to or entertain offers from other great companies.

Take a lesson from Chad, Jawed, and Steve.

Chad Hurley landed a job at PayPal as the company's fifteenth employee (and first graphic designer) in 1999, shortly after the company was founded. In fact, Hurley designed the PayPal logo at his job interview. Steve Chen was attending the University of Illinois but headed to the West Coast in 1998 to help launch the company that became PayPal. Jawed Karim also left the University of Illinois to head west and join the company.

In 2002 eBay bought PayPal, and the three received substantial bonuses. Three years later they founded YouTube in order to share videos from a dinner party with friends. In October of 2006 YouTube was sold to Google for $1.65 billion. Fortunately, the three didn't limit their base of interest. With their skills they could have easily gotten jobs with more established or bigger-name companies. PayPal was magical for them...but even more magical was the relationship they formed at PayPal that manifested itself into a brilliant venture called YouTube.

You never know who you are going to meet that will end up changing your life.

Secret #5: Don't Expect Things to Always Go Smoothly—Good Things Take Time

I was born and raised in Illinois. On our license plates is the phrase "Land of Lincoln." As I grew up, I became fascinated with Honest Abe, our sixteenth president. My great-great-grandfather was in Ford's Theatre the night Lincoln was shot. As a kid I went to Springfield, Illinois, with my family and visited Lincoln's tomb. Lincoln became somewhat of a (nonsports) hero to me.

One of the things that helped me get through some early challenges was Lincoln's life story. He had less than one year of formal schooling. A voracious reader, he was largely self-taught. Few have ever bounced back from adversity as he did and gone on to achieve so much. Here is the proof:

- 1831—Lost his job
- 1832—Defeated in run for Illinois state legislature at age twenty-three
- 1833—Failed in business
- 1835—Sweetheart died
- 1836—Had nervous breakdown
- 1838—Defeated in run for Illinois house speaker
- 1843—Defeated in run for US Congress
- 1848—Lost reelection after he was elected to Congress in 1846
- 1849—Rejected for land officer position
- 1854—Defeated in run for US Senate
- 1856—Defeated in run for vice president

- 1858—Defeated in run for US Senate
- 1860—Elected president

Don't expect things to always go smoothly. Good things take time.

Secret #6: Find Your Passion—Let It Fuel Your Future

How do you get to be the "Chairman of the Board"?

When he was nine years old, Tony Hawk's brother, Steve, gave Tony a blue fiberglass banana board. By the time Tony was fourteen, he was a professional skateboarder. At age sixteen, he was the best skateboarder in the world—winning 73 of 103 professional skateboarding contests while finishing second in 19 other ones. At seventeen, as a senior in high school, he was financially able to buy a house.

At the end of 1999, at the age of thirty-one, he retired from competitive skating, as he had accomplished a lifelong goal: to land the first-ever nine hundred (two and a half midair spins) at the X Games.

It was then that life really began in the world of Tony Hawk. Today, located just north of San Diego, is Tony Hawk Inc. Tony is in charge of this multimillion-dollar business, which boasts a group of employees who continue to think outside the box... just as Tony always has. Since his retirement, he has developed the following projects:

- In 1999 Activision and Tony created Tony Hawk's *Pro Skater* video game for PlayStation. This game and his subsequent video games continue to be best sellers.
- The Boom Book HuckJam Tour began in 2002. It is a three-hundred-city tour that appears in various sports arenas and features daredevil skateboarders, bicyclists, and motocross riders.
- He started the Tony Hawk Foundation in 2003. To date, the foundation has given over two million dollars to nonprofit organizations to help fund four hundred skate parks in poor neighborhoods throughout the country.
- In 2007, Six Flags amusement parks introduced the Tony Hawk Big Spin roller coaster.
- His 900 Films production company has produced programs for ESPN and other major sports networks.
- Hawk Clothing Company apparel is sold at Kohl's and Quicksilver stores.
- In 2008, the dream continued as Tony created a partnership with T-Mobile USA.

The passion that began over thirty years earlier in a nine-year-old boy fueled a future that no one could have imagined. Tony Hawk earned the title "Chairman of the Board" in more ways than one!

In Conclusion

There you go—six simple secrets that help you make the transition from "backpacks to briefcases." The good news is that the briefcase world really can be more fun than the backpack world. Not only does the briefcase world pay you, it can lead to your meeting some of the most interesting people on the planet.

You are about to enter the big ocean of life. Undoubtedly, you will run into some sharks, you will meet some clown fish, and you might get confused when you don't land that whale of a job.

Forget the fact that you are a little fish in a big ocean. Several of the secrets we've shared with you will be just as applicable forty years from now as they are today. Regardless of how you did in school yesterday, the last four secrets will help you use drive, determination, patience, and commitment so that you set yourself apart from the rest of the school of fish!

EPILOGUE

Enjoy the Ride!

Know Thyself

As you venture into your career, you'll find life is full of slippery slopes. Not all decisions are cut and dry, black and white. Never be afraid to go against the grain if you know it's the right thing to do. Create your own path based on your virtues and morale compass.

The famous Greek aphorism, "Know thyself," in its unique simplicity, delivers a powerful message. It suggests individuals must first truly understand themselves, their behaviors, their ambitions, and their morals in order to grasp the world around them. We live very dynamic lives, constantly changing and adapting to the environment, and we are uniquely faced with a host of opportunities. The magnitude of these opportunities can be intimating. By having an idea of what you want, you will be more adept at making the right decisions and selecting the right path for you.

Professional responsibility and ethics are a hugely important topic. In some ways, they aren't much different than what you deal with in college. In school, if you cheat just a little on an assignment, cut a corner or bend the truth, you may wind up failing a class or getting expelled from your university. Neither option sounds too appealing, but you're really only affecting your own well-being. However, once you're in the "real world", bending the truth on a company's financial statements, for example, will get you fired and possibly land you a seat in the big house. Now you've impact you life, your family, you colleagues, and the lives of your client. That said, take time to think about defining your personal and professional values. Determine how these ideals will impact your future decisions.

Life Is Not a Straight Line

You'll find in life that many people try to plot their lives out in straight lines: go to college, get a job, get married, buy a house, have kids, etc. But in reality, our lives zigzag back and forth as we encounter life's challenges and opportunities. Ask a twenty-five-year-old, a thirty-five-year-old, and a forty-five-year-old about their lives, their careers, and their daily decisions. You'll begin to see the different paths people have chosen. These differences are a result of an individual's personal choices. Remember, you control your life; you determine your own path!

Throughout this book we talked a lot about setting goals and developing a plan to achieve them. While those are important, we leave you a final thought. Enjoy the journey. Life is too short not to have fun along the way!

We wish you all the best. Good luck!

Freshman Year Goals

Sophomore Year Goals

Junior Year Goals

Senior Year Goals

Notes

Notes

Notes

Made in the USA
Lexington, KY
26 September 2017